JOHN PAUL II

Speaks to Religious

1987-1988

Book V

Dean of the Faculty of Canon Law at the Gregorian University in Rome and Consultor for various Congregations and Commissions of the Roman Curia, Father Jean Beyer, of the Society of Jesus, is also known for his many works on consecrated life.

This compilation of the texts of John Paul II follows the four volumes published in 1981, 1984, 1986 and 1988, which presented his allocutions to religious during the years 1978-1980 (Book I), 1981-1982 (Book II), 1983-1984 (Book III), and 1985-1986 (Book IV).

JOHN PAUL II
SPEAKS TO RELIGIOUS
BOOK V

PRINCIPAL ALLOCUTIONS AND LETTER
from February 1987 to December 1988

Compiled and arranged with a Synopsis
by Father Jean Beyer, S.J.

DISTRIBUTORS

LITTLE SISTERS OF THE POOR

601 Maiden Choice Lane
Baltimore, MD 21228
U.S.A.

77 Manor Road
Stoke Newington
London N16 5BL
Great Britain

Sybil Hill Road
Raheny
Dublin 5
Ireland

Market Street
P.O. Box 246
Randwick, N.S.W. 2031
Australia

INTRODUCTION

This fifth volume—published with the collaboration of the Little Sisters of the Poor, whom we here wish to thank—groups the allocutions and letter addressed to religious by Pope John Paul II during 1987-1988. It illustrates the importance that the Sovereign Pontiff attaches to the fidelity of religious Institutes to their charisms, and the apostolic activity of religious sisters, brothers, and priests.

Their consecrated life, as a result of their total gift which is offered, like the Eucharist, for the salvation of the world, deepens and extends the work of redemption, thus making it present by the power of the Spirit.

The welcome given to the preceding volumes is a sign and an encouragement. They encourage a deeper doctrinal study, as important for continued formation as for the first initiation into religious life.

The synopses of the different volumes allow us not only to take note of the richness of this pontifical teaching, but also to see its evolution and its depth.

What is said about consecrated life in religious Institutes sheds light on all consecrated life, lived individually or in community. This contribution is all the more enlightening today, as the Church experiences the birth of not only new religious Institutes, but also numerous other groups dedicated to consecrated life.

Let us note in particular the Pope's statements on the subject of vocation as a divine initiative, as a call to the consecration of one's life, a call of love and of predilection, a call which gives rise to consecration to God through the evangelical counsels, that consecration which, renewed each day, becomes the soul of every consecrated life and of every apostolate.

The response to this call finds in Mary a unique model, in a "fiat" lived out throughout her life.

The Pope is not insensitive to the problem of vocations, and the urgency of promoting them, while at the same time not becoming discouraged by their present diminution. Perhaps this diminution emphasizes the need to return to the special charism of each Institute. The straightforward, clear, and visible witness of religious here is very important; it must correspond to the expectations of youth, to their attraction to a more demanding, poorer, more solitary life, more silent and at the same time more committed, to a mission which is lived out and supported by a strengthened contemplative life.

In reading the recent texts of John Paul II, we find him taking up again his previous teachings, but we notice also his preoccupation with a more committed life, a more visible witness by religious in the Church as well as in society, and activity more faithful to one's specific charism, an activity which must be strongly integrated into the apostolate of the local Church in order to better serve the universal Church.

We cannot give a complete overview of this pontifical teaching here. In rereading the texts, in studying them according to the themes proposed in the synopsis, we cannot help but deepen our understanding of consecrated life. Religious will find here a source of fidelity and heightened esteem for the gratuitous gift of the divine call and the response it calls forth: the total gift of self to God for the salvation of the world.

Jean Beyer, S.J.

INFORMATION CONCERNING THE SYNOPSIS

The outline and chapter headings (**in Roman numerals**) of the present Synopsis are identical to those found in the Synopses of the four preceding books.

Certain topics which appeared in the preceding Synopses have not been repeated; others are new (*printed in italics*), and correspond to other aspects of religious and sacerdotal life emphasized by John Paul II during the years 1987 and 1988.

For this reason, the numbering of the topics (**Arabic numerals in bold type appearing at the left hand margin**) does not follow exactly the outline of the preceding Synopses.

For each topic, one or several numbers (in regular type) refer the reader to the corresponding paragraphs of the allocutions and letter of this present book.

Information concerning footnotes:
Book IV (Beyer, Book IV) refers to *"John Paul II Speaks to Religious, 1985-1986."*

The translations of these texts were taken, for the most part, from the *English Edition of L'Osservatore Romano*. Revisions and additions were made by translating texts from the *French Edition of L'Osservatore Romano* and *Jean-Paul II aux Religieuses et Religieux 1987-1988* —Tome V; one allocution was translated in its entirety from these same sources.

SYNOPSIS
of the Principal Allocutions and Letter of JOHN PAUL II to Religious 1987-1988

Father Jean Beyer, S.J.

ALLOCUTIONS AND LETTER

1987

1988

PERSONS ADDRESSED

A. To the Plenary Session of the Congregation for Religious and for Secular Institutes:
408-417.

B. To the Conferences of Superiors:
110-119; 191-200.

C. To Religious Institutes:
1. Camillians: 101-109.
2. Cistercian Monks and Nuns of the Strict Observance: 177-184.
3. Hospitaller Brothers of Saint John of God: 101-109; 402-407.
4. Brothers of Christian Instruction of Ploërmel: 185-190.
5. Montfort Missionaries: 129-132.
6. Passionists: 394-401.

D. To Priests and Men and Women Religious:
20-40; 201-214; 281-293; 294-299; 323-340.

E. To Priests, Men and Women Religious and Laity:
64-89; 341-351; 352-367; 368-383.

F. To Men and Women Religious:
1-19; 159-176; 257-280; 386-393.

G. To Women Religious:
42-63; 90-100; 215-237; 238-256; 310-322.

H. To Cloistered Religious:
40; 120-128; 235; 243-244; 337.

I. To Members of Secular Institutes:
41; 61; 257-280; 300-309.

J. To Seminarians and Novices:
133-158; 339; 384-385.

SYNOPSIS

I - MAGISTERIUM OF JOHN PAUL II

1. Reference to his allocutions to religious: 312, 414.
2. Reference to other documents:
   a) Redemptor Hominis: 81, 83.
   b) Dives in Misericordia: 55, 56.
   c) Dominum et Vivificantem: 24, 25, 69, 71, 81.
   d) Redemptoris Mater: 131, 212, 217, 221, 237, 240, 255, 256, 257, 267, 280, 320.
   e) Sollicitudo rei socialis: 224, 249, 373.
   f) Catechesi Tradendae: 22, 85.
   g) Redemptionis Donum: 7, 15, 42, 47, 48, 57, 62, 80, 84, 127, 273, 310, 313, 319, 346, 380, 417.
   h) Reconciliatio et Paenitentia: 32.
   i) Letter to the Bishops for Holy Thursday 1980: 139, 344.
   j) *Marian Year Letter to Consecrated Persons:* 331.
   k) Other documents or allocutions: 49, 318, 322, 325, 412.
3. Continuity with Paul VI:
   a) Evangelii Nuntiandi: 30, 74, 77, 79, 220, 247, 342, 372, 378.
   b) Evangelica Testificatio: 235, 350.
   c) Mutuae Relationes: 370, 379, 416.
   d) Motu proprio Ecclesiae Sanctae: 183.
4. Deepening awareness of the Council:
   a) Sacrosanctum Concilium: 64, 159.
   b) Dei Verbum: 24.
   c) Lumen Gentium: 35, 49, 57, 58, 63, 73, 75, 81, 118, 131, 144, 155, 156, 161, 164, 170, 218, 219, 228, 230, 238, 243, 257, 265, 267, 268, 278, 316, 321, 336, 340, 344, 368, 409.
   d) Gaudium et Spes: 39, 56, 65, 227, 235, 243, 377, 403.
   e) Presbyterorum Ordinis: 33, 140, 141, 142, 145, 291, 326, 327, 330, 345, 358.
   f) Optatam Totius: 144.

II - PARTICULAR CHARISM OF EACH INSTITUTE

III - CHARISM AND ECCLESIAL LIFE

IV - CONSECRATION

22. Consecration of life: 59, 197, 234, 239, 246.
23. Consecration and Baptism: 73-75, 147, 169, 196, 241, 262-266, 368.
24. Consecration and the Eucharist: 150, 218, 393.
25. Consecration to God: 9, 105, 152, 238, 241, 271.
26. Consecration to Jesus Christ: 75, 239, 246.
27. *Consecration through the Spirit:* 282.
28. Trinitarian consecration: 222.
29. Consecration through the profession of the counsels: 8, 147, 196, 239, 265.

V - NATURE OF CONSECRATION THROUGH THE COUNSELS

30. New and particular consecration: 196.
31. Consecration, an act of love: 53, 147, 323.
32. Exclusive and irrevocable consecration: 239.
33. Following of Christ: 45-47, 195, 222, 234, 390.
34. *Participation in Christ's consecration, in his Paschal Mystery:* 75, 79, 84, 264-265, 267, 331, 382, 390.
35. Exclusive belonging to God: 14, 42, 84, 368.
36. Total gift: 6, 8, 188, 196, 198, 238, 241, 380.
37. New life in Jesus Christ: 169, 240, 266-267, 331-332.
38. According to a personal charism: 7, 123, 260.
39. Source of freedom and fulfillment of the person: 91, 92, 94, 95, 97-98, 239, 254, 255, 368, 389.
40. *Openness to God:* 392.

VI - CONSECRATED LIFE, THEOLOGICAL LIFE

41. Life in God: 127, 260-261, 266, 268, 272-273.
42. Primacy of God: 51, 114, 411.
43. Faith, hope, charity: 175, 187, 278, 371.
44. Faith: 19, 24, 73, 108, 208-209, 217, 245-246, 248, 351.
45. Hope and confidence: 6, 70, 85, 89, 118, 169, 199, 220, 287, 290-291, 293, 298-299, 351.
46. Charity, love: 53, 66, 92, 108, 121, 128, 147, 169, 195, 198, 222, 225, 228, 265, 271, 323, 392.
47. *Charity, justice, mercy:* 55, 56, 117, 173, 249.

XII – ACTION AND CONTEMPLATION

XIII – TYPES OF APOSTOLIC ACTION

XIV - TYPOLOGY OF CONSECRATED LIFE

XV - EREMITICAL LIFE

XVI- CENOBITICAL LIFE, CONTEMPLATIVE LIFE

XVII - CLOISTERED RELIGIOUS

XVIII - RELIGIOUS PRIESTS

XIX - RELIGIOUS BROTHERS

XX - RELIGIOUS MISSIONARIES

164. Witness of missionaries and the blossoming of native vocations: 336.

XXI – MISSIONARY LIFE

165. The ministry of Peter: 21, 371.
166. Entire Church is missionary: 76-77, 83, 88, 131, 269.
167. *Promoting native vocations, signs of ecclesial maturity:* 233, 336, 377, 381.
168. *Promoting vocations of religious brothers:* 338.
169. Necessary presence of the contemplative life: 337, 383.
170. Inculturation, *respect and purification of authentic values:* 233, 332, 335, 359-361, 369, 372, 377, 407.
171. Leads to ecclesial maturity: 354-356, 372.
172. *Forming and supporting lay collaborators:* 345.

XXII – RELIGIOUS OF APOSTOLIC LIFE

173. Religious and the *identity and vocation proper to women:* 213, 221, 255, 310, 311, 312, 313-318.
174. Spiritual motherhood: 110.
175. *New relationships in faith:* 317-318, 321.
176. Religious and human fraternity, *religious and the "civilization of love":* 111, 192, 310, 312, 318.
177. *Signs of the maternal presence of Mary:* 213, 312, 380.
178. *Mary, model of the consecrated woman:* 93, 236, 256, 321-322.
179. Servants of the poor and the suffering: 225, 251.
180. Educators: 226, 254, 319.
181. Religious missionaries, *religious and inculturation:* 335-336.

XXIII – SOCIETIES OF APOSTOLIC LIFE

XXIV – RELIGIOUS LIFE: ESSENTIAL ELEMENTS

182. *Divine initiative:* 146-147, 164, 195, 260-261, 323, 362.
183. Specific charism: 10, 110, 155, 346.
184. *Search for perfect charity:* 151, 152, 265.

185. Following of Christ: 42, 45, 59-60, 195, 222, 234, 241, 265, 390.
186. Consecration essential to this state: 9, 112, 196, 238, 247, 331.
187. Public profession of the three counsels, through the vows: 8, 47-48, 79, 168, 195, 240, 392.
188. Fourth vow: 103, 402.
189. *Rooted in a particular Institute:* 381.
190. Community life in fraternal communion: 16-17, 98, 111, 168, 223, 365, 381.
191. Spirit of the Beatitudes: 48-49, 123, 170, 238, 265, 378, 389.
192. Community apostolate: 199, 365.
193. Personal and liturgical life of prayer: 14, 105, 149-150, 173, 216-218.
194. Listening and meditating on the Word of God: 216-218.
195. Life centered on the Eucharist: 150, 206-207, 218, 245, 393.
196. Religious habit: 17, 347, 399.
197. Public witness: 17, 44, 148, 332, 346-347.
198. "Sign of contradiction": 10, 48, 170.
199. Prophetic mission, *prophetic sign:* 46-47, 96, 111, 117-118, 222, 282, 298-299, 331.
200. *Sign of evangelical hope:* 46, 118, 169.
201. "Eschatological sign," *sign of the Kingdom:* 9, 118, 168, 220, 230, 239-240, 311, 349, 390, 409.
202. Sign of evangelical values: 49, 227-228, 313.
203. *Sign of the Absolute of God:* 242-243, 316, 378.
204. *Sign of God's presence: 159.*

XXV – EXIGENCIES OF RELIGIOUS LIFE

205. Contemplative dimension: 51-52, 113-114, 234, 291-292.
206. Prayer and spiritual vitality: 137, 138, 149, 216, 225, 234, 252.
207. *Total detachment:* 9.
208. Evangelical radicalism: 121, 148, 168, 266, 347.
209. Seeking after holiness: 31, 365.

XXVI - RULE AND CONSTITUTIONS

XXVII - SICK AND INFIRM RELIGIOUS

XXVIII - ECCLESIAL VALUE OF THE RELIGIOUS LIFE

XXIX – RELIGIOUS LIFE AND SECULAR CLERGY

XXX – RELIGIOUS SUPERIORSHIP

XXXI – NEW FORMS OF RELIGIOUS LIFE

XXXII – RENEWAL: ITS EXIGENCIES

XXXIII - PRESENT DANGERS AND DIFFICULTIES IN RELIGIOUS LIFE

XXXVIII – FORMATION AND FIDELITY

XXXIX – THOSE IN CHARGE OF FORMATION

XL – GOALS OF FORMATION

XLI - PRIESTHOOD

XLII - MISSION OF THE PRIESTHOOD

XLIII – BISHOPS AND PRIESTS

XLIV – PRIESTLY SPIRITUALITY

XLV – PRIESTLY VOCATION

XLVI – SECULAR INSTITUTES

JOHN PAUL II
Speaks to Religious
Principal Allocutions and Letter
1987-1988

1

TO MEN AND WOMEN RELIGIOUS IN ROME

February 2, 1987

1. *"Lift up, O gates, your lintels"* (Ps 23 [24]:9).

Today's liturgy sings the praises of the temple: the Temple of Jerusalem, first of all, and then all the others. However, the Temple of Jerusalem is the prototype here. This praise comes from the history of Israel, the Chosen People of God, from the people to whom God was particularly close through the presence of his patriarchs, through Moses and the prophets. The *Temple of Jerusalem* includes the whole tradition of this intimacy and the history of the Chosen People.

"Lift up, O gates, your lintels!" God, who lives in the heights, *came down in a cloud*. The Lord of hosts, the King of glory. The cloud of the Lord covered Moses and the Ark of the Covenant, while he still dwelt in the tent. Then he came down into the Temple, to the place called the "Holy of Holies." No one could go in except the High Priest, once a year, on the Day of Atonement.

2. *Today, the One who is Lord of the Temple comes in humble state*. He comes from among the people; even more, from the poorest among the people; He comes as a child on the fortieth day after his birth: on the day the Law prescribed for the purification of the mother and the presentation of the firstborn son.

He comes *unannounced*. Mary and Joseph bring him, just as so many other children were brought on the fortieth day after their birth.

The prophet Malachi had, without doubt, spoken of him when he asked, "But who will endure the day of his coming, and who can stand when he appears?" (Mal 3:2).

The psalmist had spoken of him when he sang: "Lift

up, O gates, your lintels...let him enter, the King of glory!"

However, everything goes on in a normal way. The Temple is silent and prays, as usual. It is pervaded as it has always been, for centuries past, by the mystery of the presence of the God of the Covenant, the God who comes from on high.

The Temple seems not to be expecting another coming.

3. *Nevertheless, there is one man who has understood.* A pair of eyes that have seen. A voice that has cried out. He has broken the silence of the Temple and made his exclamation heard.

The words of this old man are disturbing. They are full of the Holy Spirit.

In the words of Simeon there is the encounter between the old and the new; between the promise and its fulfillment. By means of this voice, God comes down into the heart of his people. He lifts up the gates of eternal destinies, and opens his earthly tabernacle to the final accomplishment in eternity. In the City of God. In the heavenly Jerusalem.

There is only one High Priest: *the Priest of future blessings*, who with his Body and his Blood *will enter the eternal sanctuary*, the Holy of Holies of heaven.

4. This, on the other hand, is the *beginning of his entrance*. Precisely today. Precisely in this presentation of the Firstborn, *which announces the final and eternal sacrifice*.

To the Jerusalem Temple comes the One who became "like his brothers in all things, so that he could be a merciful and faithful high priest before God on their behalf, to expiate the sins of the people" (Heb 2:17).

This is exactly what the eyes of the old man Simeon see. This is what his words express. This is also what is expressed, although in different words, by *Anna*, *"daughter of Phanuel...she had seen many days"* (Lk 2:36). "Coming on the scene at this moment, she gave thanks to God and talked about the child to all who looked forward to the deliverance of Jerusalem" (Lk 2:38).

"She was constantly in the Temple, worshiping day and night in fasting and prayer" (Lk 2:37).

5. *Your vocation*, dear brothers and sisters, *is derived from the testimony of Simeon and Anna*. It follows from it in a special way, and hence you come together today in this manifold community of the Orders and Congregations *in Rome*. Indeed, in a certain way, you could be said to represent all religious of the Church throughout the world.

6. Your vocation, in fact, bears certain similarities to those of Simeon and Anna: like them, called by the Holy Spirit, you have recognized the Lord to whom you have given yourselves in prayer and sacrifice: like them, after coming to know the Lord, you speak about him to the people who are waiting for salvation.

Along with Simeon you can repeat: "My eyes have witnessed your saving deed displayed for all the peoples to see, a revealing light to the Gentiles, the glory of your people Israel" (Lk 2:30-32).

7. As it was for him, your vocation also is born of the light which is Christ. Your urge to follow the way of the evangelical counsels is born of the interior encounter with the redemptive love of Christ; it is through this love that you have been called.

When, having fixed his gaze upon you, Christ began to love you, his love was directed towards each one of you individually, and it took on at the same time, a "nuptial" character: it became a love of election which *fully embraces your whole being, soul, body, thoughts and desires*, in the unrepeatable unity of the personal "I" (cf. *Redemptionis Donum,* 3).

8. Certainly, all Christians have been redeemed gratuitously by Christ and have been called to confess him before men, but you, through poverty, chastity

and obedience, have chosen *to give yourselves fully to your great and sovereign Lord*, to his will and to his love. In a short while, in the course of this liturgical assembly, you will renew in public the promises of your profession, to testify to the absolute love with which Christ has loved you and to reaffirm your absolute determination to serve him in your brothers.

9. Christians, involved in a variety of social activities in the world of today, need to have before their eyes the witness of religious, to remind them, through the commitment of total consecration to God, that the image of *this world is passing*. That is the nature of the total detachment which you have chosen and accepted and which you must maintain, finding your support in the Lord alone.

10. You know it very well: in order to offer this witness, which the world, moreover, awaits, religious life must *preserve its own particular nature*, and every Institute *must carefully protect its own charism*, desired by the Founder. Therein lies the "sign of contradiction," using Simeon's words, not *against mankind*, certainly, but against the inhuman attitudes of today's society; not against the values of the modern world but rather to bring about its salvation.

11. The evangelical animation of the world is also contributed to by that special form of consecrated life which is proper to secular Institutes, officially recognized by Pope Pius XII in the Apostolic Constitution *Provida Mater Ecclesia*, exactly forty years ago on February 2, 1947.

12. You, religious, constitute *one of the greatest treasures of the Church*, which needs your presence. Thanks be to God, that presence is not lacking in Rome, which has the greatest number of religious of any diocese in the world. There are more than twenty-five thousand in

the diocese, with three hundred and thirty generalates and over three hundred provincial houses or houses for procurators.

13. Your role in the diocese is of the utmost importance: your special style of living the Christian message is particularly useful for sustaining the commitment of the Church. I hope that your service will be especially oriented towards the preparation of the Roman Synod, from which we would all like to see results in renewal and works of charity.

14. This support which you offer to the Church comes, first of all, from the awareness that you belong to God himself in Jesus Christ, the Redeemer of the world and Spouse of the Church. He has placed his own mark upon you: in your hearts, in your minds, on your words and your actions. This loving knowledge of Christ is realized and deepened every day more and more, thanks to the life of prayer—personal, community and liturgical—proper to each religious family.

15. The religious among you who are totally dedicated to *contemplation* offer substantial help and stimulating support to their brothers and sisters who are called to an active apostolate (cf. *Redemptionis Donum,* 8). Turning trustfully to these souls dedicated to contemplation, I warmly invite them to remain unfailingly attached to this *privileged vocation*, to accept its demands of daily immolation, in the certainty that they render an irreplaceable service to the Church for the evangelization and the salvation of souls.

16. In today's world, torn by indifference, division, hatred and oppression, *fraternal communion* founded on love is an eloquent example of universal reconciliation in Christ (cf. *Code of Canon Law*, can. 602).

Carefully cultivate this fraternal love; let your houses

always be oases of peace and welcome, without exclusion or differences, in the generous acceptance of the daily self-denial which a climate of authentic fraternal life demands.

17. People today are especially sensitive to this kind of witness to fraternal love, lived authentically; it is also a convincing invitation to young people to join you on the path you have chosen.

The modern city, where the sense of the sacred is considerably diminished, needs to find people who are inspired by faith and love; it is not indifferent to a message that is clearly identifiable. Therefore, do not hesitate to *manifest your consecration in a visible way, by wearing your religious habit*, simple and poor; it is a silent but eloquent testimony. It is a sign that the secularized world needs to find along its way.

18. I am fully aware of the concern of your Institutes *to be close to the poor*, in whom you recognize the person of Christ himself: I rejoice in this and congratulate you for it. However, *only those who really know poverty and have lived it* will be able to understand the poor and help them. By your religious profession you have freely renounced the goods of this world. Therefore, it is very important that you be detached from these goods and that you avoid, as individuals and communities, the exaggerated seeking of comforts and expensive means of living. It is impossible to live poorly without feeling the pinch of poverty. Hence, I suggest that you take a look at your lives from time to time from this point of view.

19. May Mary always be the model par excellence of your life consecrated in chastity, poverty and obedience! May she watch over you, protect you, and help you to show the world the infinite love of God for all mankind.

"A revealing *light* to the Gentiles, the glory of your people Israel" (Lk 2:32).

"A sign that will be opposed, so that the thoughts of many hearts may be laid bare" (Lk 2:34-35).

We are holding the lighted candles in our hands.

Today, may they give *witness to the One who is the light of the world*. May they speak of the light which, with his coming, was also lit in the temple of our hearts: the light of faith, the light of vocation!

May they turn also to Mary, just like Simeon, on the day of the Presentation of Jesus. Is it not appropriate that she, so profoundly present to the mystery of Christ and of the Church, should know in a particular way the "thoughts of our hearts"?

2

TO PRIESTS AND CONSECRATED PERSONS IN MONTEVIDEO (URUGUAY)

March 31, 1987

20. Many times I have thought of you, your work of evangelization, and your efforts to bring the message of Christ to the men and women of your beloved country. Finding myself here among you in this metropolitan cathedral of Montevideo, I feel a deep joy; for this I continue to thank God.

I am particularly pleased, even though on this occasion I shall remain but a short time in your country, that this first meeting has been arranged. It enables me to express to you my affection, and to tell you personally how much I appreciate your generous and irreplaceable collaboration in the great work of the new evangelization of this country, a country which the Pope loves so much, and which is a source of great hope throughout the entire Church in Latin America.

21. For the first time, the Successor of Peter comes to visit you. May the Lord grant that this special moment be an occasion to confirm you in the faith and strengthen in you the ties of intimate communion with the Apostolic See, with your bishops and with your many brothers and sisters throughout the entire world. They are united with you in the consoling mystery of the Mystical Body of Christ; even though they do not know you, they love you and pray for you as you do for them. The visible foundation of this unity is the ministry of Peter; thus was it willed by Christ himself and experienced by you and by so many children of the Church whom I meet on my missionary journeys. (...)

22. It gives me particular satisfaction to know that you are committed to a special effort of evangelization, to

promote the "parish mission" in each and every one of the dioceses of Uruguay. Traditionally, this is an irreplaceable means for the periodic and vigorous renewal of Christian life (cf. *Catechesi Tradendae,* 47). Therefore, I encourage you to prepare this mission with enthusiasm, generosity and evangelical courage, in an atmosphere of perfect unity and communion with your bishops so that, with the help of God, you will achieve the objectives which you set for yourselves, following the way set out by Puebla (cf. nos. 165-339): to transmit, through multiple channels, the truth about Christ, the Church and mankind to all the men and women of Uruguay, as a message of salvation which transforms hearts and the entire society.

23. The ever vital mandate of the divine Master echoes in our ears: "Go, therefore, and teach all peoples to observe all that I have commanded you" (cf. Mt 28:19-20). Aware of such great responsibility, you must feel the same apostolic urgency as Saint Paul when he said, "Woe to me if I do not preach the Gospel" (1 Cor 9:16). As the same apostle recommends, you must preach the word "in season and out of season" (2 Tim 4:2), fully convinced of the inherent strength of the truth which the Church has professed for the last two thousand years.

24. All evangelization is thus orientated towards having every person and every community open itself fully to the Word of God. "Faith in its deepest essence is the openness of the human heart to the gift, to God's self-communication in the Holy Spirit" (*Dominum et Vivificantem,* 51). The Church will be infinitely grateful to you if you never tire of helping your brothers to receive the divine Word just as it is: revealed and inspired by God, his initiative and gift, preached by the Church, celebrated in the liturgy and lived by the saints. Only in this way will your communities be able to "reread" the Word of God in an authentic way in the face of new events. "The Holy Spirit constantly perfects faith by his gifts, so that Revelation may be more and more profoundly understood" (*Dei Verbum,* 5).

25. As with all local Churches, your Church can point with legitimate pride to eloquent monuments like this cathedral; they are reminders of the effectiveness of this evangelical power and truth in your country. I refer, among others, to persons who have figured prominently throughout your history: the first Vicar Apostolic, Damaso Antonio Larranaga, whose name you gave to your recently-erected Catholic University of Uruguay; your first bishop, the Servant of God, Msgr. Jacinto Vera, a zealous and exemplary pastor; and that great teacher and thinker, Msgr. Mariano Soler, first archbishop of this ecclesiastical province. The example and enduring work of these and many other famous names of the Church in Uruguay cannot be forgotten. Today more than ever it is necessary to raise the torch of the Gospel truth to illuminate the path of our many brethren who are uncertain and hopelessly drifting. The Church's route is that person in whose heart "the Holy Spirit does not cease to be the guardian of hope" (*Dominum et Vivificantem,* 67).

26. However, we must not forget that this effective and transforming power of the revealed word does not come from the human eloquence with which it is proclaimed, but rather from its inherent truth, that is, from its authenticity as the Word of God. It is the Master himself who, in passing on the message received from the Father, feels the need to emphasize that he is acting in complete fidelity to his divine source: "The word which you hear is not mine but the Father's who sent me" (Jn 14:24).

27. The Gospel message is not *authentic* and thus is not able to renew Christian life profoundly if it is not proclaimed in all its purity and integrity. It is necessary therefore to overcome the temptation to reduce the Gospel to certain passages, interpreted according to one's own likes and opinions or in the light of preconceived ideological positions.

Do not let yourselves be discouraged in the face of an apparent failure in your apostolate. Rather, let us listen to the voice of Christ who continues to say to us, as he said to his apostles: "Put out into the deep and let down your nets for a catch" (Lk 5:4). Yes, as true apostles, let us lift up our eyes to the Lord in our moments of anxiety and say to him, "We trust you, and in your name we will continue to let down our nets; even at the cost of sacrifice and misunderstanding, we must proclaim without fear, adaptations or ambiguities the complete and authentic truth about your person, about the Church you founded, about mankind and about the world you have redeemed by your blood."

28. We do not find the criteria for our teaching and our conduct in purely sociological, psychological or political facts, but in faith, in our communion of life with Christ and in complete fidelity to the Church's teaching.

Remember, dear brothers and sisters, that if you do not offer these specific lights which shine forth from the Gospel alone, you differ in little or nothing from other analysts and social workers. If those who hear you observe that your vision does not go beyond secular horizons, they will ask themselves in astonishment where, and in what, can the originality of your presence and your message be found. Often, fortunately, the *sensus fidei*, present in the People of God, predisposes the faithful to a ready acceptance of the true bread of the Gospel, refusing that which is adulterated.

29. Your evangelizing effort, supported by prayer and penance and enlivened by the sanctifying Spirit, must lead others to conversion, that is, to return to the truth, and to friendship with God, from whom they have separated themselves by losing his grace. Your words and your example must stimulate lukewarm Christians to change; they must encourage souls to live the spirit of the Beatitudes with joy; they must foster vocations in men and women, leading them to opt for the total consecration of their lives to the service of God and of their brothers and sisters.

30. In your apostolic work you must give priority to conversion of the heart. Why? Because from within comes all which separates a person from his Creator; here all the barriers which separate him from his brothers are built (cf. Mk 7:20-23). "The Church considers it to be undoubtedly important to build up structures which are more human, more just, more respectful of the rights of the person and less oppressive and less enslaving, but she is conscious that the best structures and the most idealized systems soon become inhuman if the inhuman inclinations of the human heart are not made wholesome, if those who live in these structures or who rule them do not undergo a conversion of heart and of outlook" (*Evangelii Nuntiandi,* 36). Here we have the core of your missionary task; here nobody can replace you because you must be prudent collaborators of the Holy Spirit, "the principal agent of evangelization" (*ibid.,* 75), in a work which, more often than not, attracts little attention and cannot be measured in purely human terms.

31. Neither success nor failure must ever cause you to forget your vocation as servants; you must allow the Lord to grant growth when and how he chooses (cf. 1 Cor 3:7). At the same time you must imitate the apostle Paul who knew how to suffer want and to live in abundance, ready for anything, for plenty or hunger, abundance or want, able to say bravely, "I can do all things in him who strengthens me" (Phil 4:12-13).

I hope that this meeting will give you a sense of urgency to correspond to the graces received; then, with renewed enthusiasm you will devote your entire capacity for love to the search for holiness, to which we have been destined by God's choice. Only if we try to identify with Christ will we be able to truly say with the apostle: "It is no longer I who live, but Christ who lives in me" (Gal 2:20). Only then will we have sufficient strength to build the "civilization of love," a world of greater solidarity, which is at the same time more human and more divine, moved by the irresistible force of charity.

32. If baptism is the decisive moment of our spiritual grafting into Christ, the new life which springs from it will need the continual sap of sacramental grace in order to develop properly. In light of the possibility of our breaking away from him, the Lord established the sacrament of Penance or Reconciliation. As you know well, the Synod of Bishops studied this most important question in 1983. In the Apostolic Exhortation *Reconciliatio et Paenitentia,* you will find the relevant pastoral directives. We should frequently approach this source of life. There, God our Father will always welcome you into his arms with love; you will find the true peace which only Christ can give and an authentic renewal in the new life of the Spirit.

33. I exhort you priests, as ministers of reconciliation, to acquire a renewed appreciation for the celebration of this sacrament in which Jesus uses you to reach the inner recesses of the heart. Continue to study and pray so as to be worthy of this ministry of reconciling people to God, possibility so unheard of that it provoked this astonished exclamation: "Who can forgive sins but God alone?" (Mk 2:7). Therefore, I ask you to be always available. Do not limit the time which you dedicate to the administration of this sacrament and to the direction of the faithful in the way of perfection. Remember that God is always waiting for the son or daughter who returns home to be pardoned and reconciled through you. Your own experience of approaching this sacrament will be the greatest stimulus to your pastoral dedication and a further reason for you to live your "Easter joy" continually (*Presbyterorum Ordinis,* 11).

34. My dear brothers and sisters, maintain a continual relationship with the divine Master, truly present in the Eucharist. Only in this way will you be able to reveal to the faithful the secret of Christian life. Jesus himself said: "He who abides in me, and I in him, he it is who bears much fruit, for apart from me you can do nothing" (Jn

15:5). Be witnesses to the love of the Eucharistic Christ, a love which spurs on to unlimited generosity and to a total gift to him, and through him, to all those who seek him with a sincere heart. How else will you discover the meaning of your consecrated life and the sense of your total surrender, without this daily intimate encounter with Christ?

It is both necessary and urgent to awaken in the faithful a veneration for this ineffable sacrament, its celebration in the Sacrifice of the Mass and its frequent reception with proper preparation. If the spiritual growth of the faithful is centered on the Eucharist, the vitality of the Church is assured. For this reason I was happy to learn that in 1988 you intend to celebrate a "Eucharistic Year." Always, but in a special way during this celebration, you must respond with your love to the eternal gift of Jesus Christ in this sacrament, model of service to our brothers and sisters. On the other hand, the Marian Year, which will soon begin, will prepare you to live in the Upper Room with Mary (Acts 1:14) and become involved as she is in Christ's redemptive sacrifice, realized in the Eucharist.

35. In recent years, what is called the "preferential option for the poor" has been emphasized with special force and insistence within the apostolic and pastoral mission of the Church. As you know, this preference, which was evidenced by the Second Vatican Council, (cf. *Lumen Gentium,* 8) was immediately and warmly welcomed by the whole Church and especially by the Church in Latin America. It could not have been otherwise, since we are dealing with the eternal message of the Gospel. Christ acted in this way (cf. Lk 4:18); so too did the apostles, and the Church has lived in this way throughout the two millennia of her history.

36. In being "preferential," this "option" nonetheless indicates and implies that it must not be exclusive or excluding. The message of salvation which Christ brought

to us is destined "for all creation" (cf. Mk 16:15). It is an "option" that has its foundation in the Word of God and not in criteria offered by human sciences or opposing ideologies, which usually reduce the poor to economic or sociopolitical categories. This "option," nonetheless, has to be fulfilled by looking at the person with an integral vision, that is to say, in his temporal and eternal vocation. It is precisely there that, in the light of Revelation, we discover that the greatest poverty of all is to be deprived of God, which is the consequence of sin. Therefore, the first liberation that Christ came to offer man is liberation from sin, from that moral evil which exists in his heart and which is itself the root and cause of oppressive structures. You will be able to approach the poor and their problems effectively, enlightening them with the Gospel, if you are humble of heart, able to receive the Word of God as it is and if you take up a life of authentic detachment, following Christ.

37. Those who, like yourselves, priests and consecrated persons, have opted unconditionally for Christ, must always be builders of unity, never of division in the name of particular ideological conceptions or of political preferences, no matter how legitimate they may be. You have the responsibility of teaching moral and ethical principles, as well as the concrete applications of those fundamental principles which must inspire economic, social and political activity, so that they may be truly "human." However, leave the care of temporal affairs to competent lay people who have well-formed moral consciences; do not take their place to the abandonment of what is specifically yours. This way of behaving does not indicate, in any way, an indifference to temporal problems, but is rather a sign of radical commitment which you have accepted for higher motives.

38. I am aware that many of you, beloved *religious and consecrated persons,* have a qualified presence in various fields of the ecclesial apostolate: in parishes and

communities, in schools and hospitals, as well as in rural areas. You work with children and young people, with the elderly and students, with the sick, the poor and the marginalized and with many other categories of people, all of them in need of material and spiritual assistance. Work with joy and enthusiasm in these services and also in the humble and least sought-after tasks which are a part of every evangelizing activity. Do not forget that the love of God passes through you, because he has chosen to need your hearts and your hands and your whole life, so as to reach out and draw close to all.

39. There are many of you who, by vocation, are dedicated to teaching at various levels from primary and secondary schools to the recently-founded Catholic University itself. The educational apostolate needs the widest support and generous collaboration of the entire local Church, so that the seed which is sown may become a fruitful tree and produce ripe and abundant fruit for the good of the entire Uruguayan society.

Your responsibility is great, in dedicating your energies to a field that is of such paramount importance for the present and the future of the life of the Church in your country. Remember that she has entrusted to you in a special manner the immense task of the evangelization of culture in a world which, on the one hand seems ever more secularized, yet on the other hand shows that without God human life is meaningless. Only a culture impregnated with Christian hope, which is able to respond to the transcendent search of the human heart, deserves the name of a "new humanism, one in which man is defined first of all by his responsibility towards his brothers and towards his history" (*Gaudium et Spes,* 55).

40. There are also present some *contemplatives* from the various monasteries which, thank God, exist in Uruguay. Know, dear daughters, that you occupy a privileged place in the heart of the Church because you, like Saint Teresa of Jesus and many other contemplative souls

are like "love in the heart of the Church." Live in the profound joy of knowing that by means of your austere and demanding life, you also evangelize "by imparting a hidden apostolic fruitfulness" (*Perfectae Caritatis,* 7). Thank you for your prayers and your generous surrender within the silence of the cloister! (...)

41. I would like to invite the consecrated persons who belong to *secular Institutes* and to *associations of apostolic life* to continue in their work of evangelization with ever renewed generosity and enthusiasm, living their consecration in the world, so as to imbue all human situations and structures with the Gospel. (...)

3

TO CONSECRATED WOMEN IN MAIPU (CHILE)

April 3, 1987

42. I am very happy to meet you in Maipú, a meaningful and important place in your country's history. In this place the nation of Chile achieved her freedom; Maipú is also the site where a very strong bond was forged with the neighboring people of Argentina. In this very place the founding fathers of the nation expressed their love for Mary and made a promise that has linked the destiny of this great country to the Mother of Jesus.

Through you, I greet all consecrated persons in religious life and the members of secular Institutes. My thoughts are also with all who are giving their lives in remote areas of this beloved land, and all those who could not be with us today because they are working in hospitals, caring for the elderly, or carrying out their self-sacrificing work in other areas of education and social assistance. I also greet the men and women religious who are infirm and who offer their suffering for the Church.

This meeting gives me an opportunity to confirm you in faith and to encourage you in your vocation to follow the Lord unconditionally with the "joy of belonging exclusively to God" (*Redemptionis Donum,* 8), since your whole existence is a spousal response to "Follow me," as a declaration of love (cf. Mk 10:21-31).

43. Following the Lord should make you more sensitive to the sufferings and needs of all men and women and, at the same time, more faithful to the Church. Consecrated life in this beloved land of Chile has taken up in a spirit of faith the pastoral directives of the bishops, thus contributing to the vitality of the apostolate and to a greater participation in the local Churches.

I support your effort to bring about the orientations of the Second Vatican Council and of the Latin American bishops in Medellin and Puebla in regard to the consecrated life. You have tried to rediscover your own charisms and have traced the roots of your Founders, adapting these to the current situations; you have also revitalized the life of prayer and community life according to the tenets of the Gospels and the tradition and teachings of the Magisterium.

44. Through your service in schools, hospitals, parishes and sharing *the life and the lot of the most needy,* you give visible witness of obedience, that is, of accepting the will of God who calls you to his service. It is only in an attitude of poverty, in being always disposed to hear the Word of God in your heart (cf. Lk 2:19,51) and in living evangelical poverty that you can approach your most outcast brothers and sisters to help them discover the Gospel message of the Beatitudes as well as to improve their conditions of life.

45. The Church's presence in the world—and I would add, here and now, in your country—presents a series of challenges that must be clearly confronted with discernment and Gospel boldness, as the fruit of an authentic personal and community renewal. Thus all apostolic activity entrusted to you demands a prior faithfulness and a generous surrender to the Word and grace of God, which will make evident the deep inspiration of your consecrated life. *Your following of Jesus must be clear and manifest* in such a way that the reference point of your way of life, scale of values and your attitudes can be none other than the person and the message of Jesus himself. He is your Guide, your Master, your Spouse, your Lord, because your lives are centered on a personal bond with him. In order to follow him and share his destiny you have left all things (cf. Mt 19:27), and thus you should make him shine forth in your words and actions.

46. It is often said that the world thirsts for the Gospel message, and in this sense it asks that religious life be prophetic. But is there anything more prophetic than a life dedicated to the Lord, to his message, to making him present among people? By being near your brother or sister, you are already a sign of *Gospel hope.*

47. In a world that strives for power and wealth, where the true human dimension of the body is losing its meaning and is separated from authentic love, profession of the *evangelical counsels in order to follow Jesus more closely* is an impressive prophecy. Before injustice and violence, and before the materialism which destroys human dignity, you, faithful to the Church, embrace a path based on the following of Christ who was poor, chaste and obedient. "The rich person is not the one who possesses, but the one who 'gives,' the one who is capable of giving" (*Redemptionis Donum,* 5).

48. This renunciation of all human pride and power defines the relations between persons and presents an alternative which must be lived in your communities, an alternative inspired by the Beatitudes. "The world needs the authentic 'contradiction' provided by religious consecration, as an unceasing stimulus of salvific renewal...(It needs) this witness of love (and)...redemption as this is imprinted upon the profession of the evangelical counsels" (*Redemptionis Donum,* 14).

49. Your life is an appeal that the future of man and of the world be orientated, starting now, to the same perspective of the values of the Kingdom. Your conduct in the midst of the world should remind humanity that the Gospel demand is still valid, that to gain life one must surrender it for love (cf. Lk 9:24). Christian witness, inseparably united to the living out of the vows and evangelical counsels, has to broaden the horizon of human aspirations and to reject all ideologies that tend to enslave

the world and mankind to the requirements of a materialistic world view. Consecrated persons "by their state in life...give splendid and striking testimony that the world cannot be transfigured and offered to God without the spirit of the Beatitudes" (*Lumen Gentium,* 31). So it is that "before all these menacing powers we decided to be poor like Christ, the Son of God and Savior of the world; poor like Francis, the eloquent image of Christ; poor like so many great souls who have shed light on the path of humanity" (*Christmas Message,* 1986).

50. In order that the religious aspect of your life be obvious and fruitful, it is important that members of the Institutes of active life take upon themselves a serious reflection in order to bring about an authentic synthesis between action and contemplation. I know that you work without rest to evangelize and serve your brothers according to the Gospel. I know that you are present in all areas of the Church. All of this demands that your apostolate be filled with God; that you work with great purity of intention and in a spirit of brotherhood and harmony without excluding anyone.

51. In order to be consecrated in the midst of daily work you must feel a deep need to find and love God in your tasks. There cannot be any conflict between your work and true contemplation. This presupposes that you work for God and through him; that you work with him and that you meet him in your work. Certainly, this also requires that you know how to set aside special moments of irreplaceable intimacy with the Lord. Contemplation leads to apostolic activity and this same work helps us appreciate the importance of time explicitly dedicated to prayer and contemplation.

52. Every consecrated person is, deep down, a *contemplative*. The Second Vatican Council teaches that Institutes of contemplative life "offer God a choice sacrifice of praise. They brighten God's people with the richest splen-

dors of sanctity. By their example they motivate this people; by imparting a hidden apostolic fruitfulness, they make this people grow" (*Perfectae Caritatis,* 7).

53. It gives me great joy to address some special words of appreciation and affection from this Marian shrine to all the contemplative sisters who live in Chile. You are truly the heartbeat of the Church; with your austere and demanding enclosed life you are true co-workers in the saving mission of Christ and a special expression of his love.

The dedication to which God has consecrated you by a special movement of his love manifests a great predilection for you. Your witness, lived in havens of peace and in the depths of the interior life, is a manifestation of love, of that spousal love which has its roots in the love of Christ. Continue, then, to proclaim with your silent and hidden lives the glory of the Most Holy Trinity, and by your prayers and witness help your brothers and sisters to reach the fullness of Christian life in the Father, the Son and the Holy Spirit.

54. The religious who belong to Institutes of active life should live in such a way that they encounter God at each moment. Jesus has to be sought and found where he awaits you, in the signs he has chosen: the Eucharist, his Word, the sacraments, the community, your brothers and sisters, in the daily events of your lives...You must be *contemplatives in your work.* This will give consistency to your lives and depth to your apostolate. The sign of authenticity in your lives, for both contemplation and apostolate, is the "unity of life" by which one always seeks the Lord and his saving will. In this harmonious synthesis of contemplation and action, you will discover that evangelization is a privileged means of sanctification and an ordinary exercise of consecrated life.

55. I wish to point out that as persons who experience in your lives the grace of reconciliation with God, you

should be at the same time *instruments of reconciliation* in the Church and in Chilean society. The freedom which the practice of the vows and evangelical counsels gives you should make you more sensitive to the problems of our time so that you can shed on these problems the saving light of the Christian message. We cannot silence the reality of sin and its consequences in the lives of individuals and of societies. Everyone can see the evil consequences of egoism, divisions, vendettas, and injustices all over the world. The Christian does not possess the immediate solution to conflicts, but does have a means to confront them with the Gospel message: forgive offenses, love your enemies, have a heart full of mercy towards everyone. In effect, "the experience of the past and of our own time demonstrates that justice alone is not enough, that it can even lead to the negation and destruction of itself, if that deeper power, which is love, is not allowed to shape human life in its various dimensions" (*Dives in Misericordia,* 12). "The Church lives an authentic life when she professes and proclaims mercy" (ibid., 13). Therefore, "the Church rightly considers it her duty and the purpose of her mission to guard the authenticity of forgiveness, both in life and behavior and in educational and pastoral work" (*ibid.,* 14).

56. The commitments of consecrated life, joyfully accepted, enroll you in that school of mercy and love that must characterize the disciples of Jesus. The theology of the cross, *especially for you, consists in transforming difficulties and suffering into love which gives itself* like Christ who lived and died loving others. In contrast to this Christian attitude there are others who propose theories that are apparently more effective at first, but which in reality inevitably unloose a spiral of violence and transform life and human living "into an arena of permanent strife between one group and another" (*Dives in Misericordia,* 14). You must be instruments of peace in the Lord's hands and believe in the truth and strength of the Gospel of reconciliation. Peace begins to become a reality

at the individual and national levels when there is "a sincere gift of self" (*Gaudium et Spes,* 24).

57. It is particularly important, dear sisters, that you live in intense *ecclesial communion.* You know that this is a sign which distinguishes the true disciples of Christ. This communion is not reduced to a juridical bond but it is rooted in the life of God who is Love. The Church participates in and shares it as an image of the divine Unity and Trinity (cf. *Lumen Gentium,* 4). Religious and consecrated persons "impelled by a love which the Holy Spirit has poured into their hearts...spend themselves ever increasingly for Christ and for his Body, the Church" (*Perfectae Caritatis,* 1). Therefore, "in the apostolate which consecrated persons exercise, their spousal love for Christ becomes as it were, in an almost organic way, love for the Church as the Body of Christ, for the Church as the People of God, for the Church which is at one and the same time both Spouse and Mother" (*Redemptionis Donum,* 15).

58. Always strive to strengthen the bonds of ecclesial communion with your pastors and try to be at all times a leaven of unity among the members of the communities. As followers of Christ you should pay special attention to those who are in more danger or who are more marginalized. May your humility and acceptance inspire them to draw close to the flock of the one Shepherd.

Consecrated persons must, through their lives of surrender and sacrifice, give witness to the Church's mission as the "sacrament" chosen by the Lord to reconcile persons among themselves and to God (cf. *Lumen Gentium,* 1). This universally valid road of reconciliation is particularly important in your country which is looking for a path of lasting peace in the midst of undeniable tensions. Your pastors have repeatedly called on all people of good will to make a great effort to construct peace and to find *ways of solidarity and reconciliation* within a legitimate pluralism. By your prayer, your witness of consecrated life and your apostolic and charitable activity you must always be builders of communion and peace.

59. In this meeting with you that I have so desired, beloved women religious of Chile, at the feet of the most holy Virgin, I wish to leave you a special watchword: *"Follow Christ radically!"* Love for his person and dedication to his redemptive work is your basic option in life. By your religious profession you have chosen him in such a radical fashion that the "unfathomable richness of Christ" (Eph 3:8) has become the center and measure of all other commitments. Only in Christ and through him can you discern and fulfill any other option, in such a way that your service to your brothers and sisters passes through your unconditional gift to Christ, your Lord and Spouse.

60. The radical following of Christ should lead you to an unreserved identification with Christ in his mystery of poverty, chastity and obedience. This and nothing else should be the most intimate and ecclesial center of the heart of the woman religious and the source of her fruitfulness in the Church and in the world. Her preferential love for Christ must animate and orientate her whole life.

The dynamism of your unconditional following of the Lord will also bring you to a renewed commitment to your *missionary effort* within and outside your country. I am glad to know that Chilean missionaries, both men and women, are already collaborating in the spread of the Gospel in other continents. In your country also, which the Lord is blessing with abundant vocations, it is important and urgent that men and women religious go to the more remote, difficult and needy areas and that they have there the necessary stability so that the work of the Church may be strengthened.

61. I wish to say a special word on this occasion to the members of *secular Institutes,* who, by their style of consecrated life, confirmed by Vatican Council II, render a valuable service to the Church in Chile; they respond to new apostolic challenges and are a leaven for Christ in the world. Your charism constitutes a service that is greatly needed at the present time. With your apostolic activity in

the world you sing the glory of God and contribute effectively to the realization of that civilization of love which is the divine plan for humanity as it awaits his coming in glory.

62. Beloved sisters, I have the joy of meeting you in this temple dedicated to Our Lady of Carmel. The Virgin continues to be the model of every consecrated person. She is the consecrated woman, the Virgin of Nazareth, who, listening, praying and loving, was chosen to be the Mother of God. "If the entire Church finds in Mary her first Model, all the more reason do you find her so—you as consecrated individuals and communities within the Church!" (*Redemptionis Donum,* 17).

63. Humble and forgetting herself, Mary gave her life so that God's will could be accomplished in her. Her very being was placed at the service of God's saving plan. Truly she was blessed and fortunate. Deprived of all power except the power of the Holy Spirit which overshadowed her, (cf. Lk 1:35), she did not flee the cross, but lived in spousal fidelity to the Lord as the figure and Mother of the Church (cf. *Lumen Gentium,* 58).

Handmaids of Christ, may the Virgin Mary always accompany you; may she teach you the path of fidelity and humble joy in giving your lives for the service of the Kingdom; may she teach you and encourage you on the road to holiness and in the work of evangelization.

4

TO CONSECRATED PERSONS AND PASTORAL WORKERS IN BUENOS AIRES

April 10, 1987

64. "Families of peoples, acclaim the Lord, acclaim the glory and the power of the Lord" (Ps 95:7).

Beloved in the Lord, the liturgy which we are celebrating today repeats these beautiful words of the psalter, which invite us to glorify God for his saving action among all peoples and throughout the entire created world.

Today this song springs forth from the hearts of those who have consecrated themselves to walk with joy along the path of perfection and make themselves totally available for the work of evangelization. Thank you for your presence here today and for your enthusiasm; thank you for your testimony which is surely translated every day into a commitment to holiness and to the apostolate.

As we are now on the threshold of Holy Week, the Church reminds us through the words of the psalmist that it is Christ who prays within us, through us and for us, as if wanting again and forever to surrender to God the entire creation and the whole of humanity, eagerly desiring that the restoration of all things in him soon become a reality, "so that God may be all in all" (1 Cor 15:28). Thus, the Lord anticipates in our lives "the hymn that is sung eternally in heaven" (*Sacrosanctum Concilium,* 83).

65. From the day of the Incarnation, Jesus, the Word made flesh, began his work of redeeming everything that was fallen due to sin, and restoring it to the Father as a new creation. Jesus, "through his incarnation united himself, in some way, to each person" (*Gaudium et Spes,* 22), and has transformed him into a new creature through the divine sonship of which he himself has made us sharers through his bloody sacrifice and glorious resurrection.

66. Indeed, the Father has sent his Son into the world so that we, united to him and transformed in him, may be able to give back to God the same gift of love which he gives us: "Yes, God loved the world so much that he gave his only Son, so that everyone who believes in him may not be lost but may have eternal life" (cf. Jn 3:16). From that gift of love, we can better understand and bring to fulfillment God's eternal life in us, making us sharers in the total and eternal surrender of the Son to the Father in the love of the Holy Spirit. This sublime reality is expressed by Saint John of the Cross in the words: "to give God himself to God in God" (*Living Flame of Love,* 3rd hymn).

67. I wanted to remind you of these Christian ideals to renew in your minds and hearts the ultimate and eminent goal of all evangelization. Only the apostle who is in love with these ideals of perfection will be able to face all difficulties, transforming them into a more radical following of Christ and a more determined pastoral commitment. "God is fully glorified from the moment that men fully and consciously accept the work of salvation which he accomplished in Christ" (*Ad Gentes,* 7), the Second Vatican Council tells us.

68. However, there is an obstacle in the heart of each person which hinders this process of interior unity and harmony with the entire creation; it is sin, the breaking away from God, enmity with one's brother or sister. We live in a society which sometimes seems to have lost its consciousness of sin, precisely because it has lost the sense of spiritual values which should animate any authentic humanism. Coming forth from the hands of the Creator, humanity can achieve its full realization only when people think and act, on both the individual and social levels, in a manner befitting our condition as an "image and likeness of God" (cf. Gen 1:26). In the final analysis, sin is the destruction of the gift of God given to us in the Spirit, through Christ the Savior.

69. Christ conquers sin with his sacrifice on the cross, his "offering of supreme love, which surpasses the evil of all the sins of men" (*Dominum et Vivificantem,* 31). Hence, he conquers through his obedience to the Father until death, which has already been transformed into the Paschal Mystery of the resurrection (cf. Phil 2:8-11). The conquest of sin through love is a new beginning of the "restoration" to God of all things and of all humanity as his. Thanks to the Paschal Mystery of Christ, everything belongs to God in an even fuller sense, as a universe that has been redeemed and restored in Christ (cf. Eph 1:10). Man as a person and all of humanity can make their own existence an offering to God and to others in Christ.

70. It is sad to acknowledge that our own sin has crucified Christ who lives in our brother and sister; yet it is consoling to encounter Christ crucified, who lovingly dies in order to destroy sin and restore humanity. The person who has been forgiven and restored, like Saint Paul or Saint Augustine, is better suited to announce forgiveness and reconciliation to all. Is it not true that Christian hope is revived in this magnificent Gospel perspective, by knowing how to make peace through the proclamation of forgiveness to all and reconciliation in the joy of the risen Christ?

71. The liturgy has been bringing us gradually closer to the celebration of Easter, the mystery of Emmanuel, God with us. Jesus Christ is the Son of God who sealed forever a covenant of love between God and man. "He dwelt among us" (cf. Jn 1:14), and shared our very existence to the extent of making his sacrificial death the source of a new life for all people (cf. Jn 7:38-39). Through Christ and in the new life of the Spirit, man can already be given back to the Most Holy Trinity, since it is from his cross that the power of redemption comes (*Dominum et Vivificantem,* 14).

72. Thanks to the redeeming death of Christ, the Son of God, the world and the entire humanity have recovered the balance that they have lost through sin, thus reestablishing the wonderful unity of the cosmos and of the whole human family. Thanks to the Paschal Mystery, the whole created world shares in the glory of the risen Christ and can sing "the new hymn" of the followers of Christ (cf. Rev 5:9), which is echoed in our liturgical celebration: "Sing to the Lord a new song, sing to the Lord all the earth, sing to the Lord and bless his name" (Ps 95:1-2).

73. As we are now gathered here together to take part in this Eucharist where the Paschal Mystery, through which Christ restored us to the Father, is realized, *all of us* direct our eyes with deep faith to our Redeemer (cf. Heb 12:2), to reaffirm in ourselves from the very depths of our hearts that *all of us* are Christ's.

We are totally his by baptism, through which we are sacramentally configured to the death and resurrection of the Lord, in order to begin a new life, by which Christ recovers and gives back to the Father our entire existence in newness of life. By our baptism we are already called to be holy, since "all the faithful," of whatever state or condition, are called to the fullness of the Christian life and the perfection of charity (*Lumen Gentium,* 40).

74. *We are totally his by the mission* which he entrusted to the apostles and to the whole Church. "It merits having the apostle consecrate all his time and all his energies, and to sacrifice, if necessary, his own life" for this mission (*Evangelii Nuntiandi,* 5).

We are totally his by the priestly ordination which enables us sacramentally to represent Christ, the Head of the Mystical Body, and thus to serve all the faithful in his name and with his authority. The fact that we have received the sacrament of Orders demands on our part a profound identification with Christ and the mysteries of our faith, of which we are the ministers.

75. *We are totally his by religious consecration* and by the permanent practice of the evangelical counsels, which, rooted in that restoration and gift to the Father which the sacrament of Baptism formed in each of us, imprints in our being a likeness to and configuration with Christ, who died and rose again. This consecration to Christ is "a sign and stimulus of love and a singular source of spiritual fertility in the world" (*Lumen Gentium,* 42).

Hence, all of us priests, consecrated persons and pastoral workers are totally his, with the paschal joy of continuing, each according to his own special calling, the presence, the word, the sacrifice and the saving action of Christ, the conqueror of sin and death.

76. Today, in this Eucharistic assembly, all of us, who are totally his, want not only to listen to his message, but, above all, to receive in our hearts the missionary command of the Lord: "Go out to the whole world; proclaim the Good News to all creation" (Mk 16:15).

This missionary mandate of Jesus is like a declaration of love, inasmuch as he entrusts to us the dearest thing he has: the command received from the Father to redeem fallen humanity. If he offered his life to bring to fulfillment his salvific mission, we who are totally his have also received this command from the Church in order to share our life with him.

77. The consecration that was realized in us through baptism is the primary source of this call to the apostolate, to evangelization. If "the whole Church is missionary, the work of evangelization is a fundamental duty of the People of God" (cf. *Ad Gentes,* 35). Because of this, "evangelization is for no one an individual or isolated act; it is one that is deeply ecclesial" (*Evangelii Nuntiandi,* 60).

78. Furthermore, those of us who have received the ministerial priesthood are, by virtue of a new title,

especially bound to undertake the work of the apostolate and that of evangelization, by means of the ministry of the Word and of the sacraments. For us, serving the evangelizing activity of the Church is a pressing obligation, though a delightful one as well. We are valid and effective instruments of the action of Christ, the Good Shepherd, in souls; we are the necessary instruments of unity for the evangelizing activity which the Lord entrusted to the Church.

79. The divine call to religious profession, to the permanent exercise of the evangelical counsels, opens new paths for the Church's apostolate, and new energies for evangelization flow from it. The consecrated person must be a transparent sign and the bearer of the offering of the world to God. He or she is also a living expression of the poverty of Christ, who renounced everything and made himself "obedient unto death, even to death on the cross" (Phil 2:8). Through this consecration to the Lord, the immolation of Christ on the altar of the Father's salvific will clearly appears. From this the mysterious apostolic fruitfulness of the consecrated life arises, an effective sign of evangelization. Those called to this consecration, who "are caught up in the dynamism of the Church's life...are eminently willing and free to leave everything and to go and proclaim the Gospel even to the ends of the earth" (*Evangelii Nuntiandi,* 69.)

80. The Gospel is proclaimed by means of living words and by life-giving deeds; however, it is especially proclaimed through the witness of a total self-giving to God, entrusting to him the entire creation in a spousal surrender to the cause of the Kingdom, which Christ has already inaugurated in the history of mankind. Christ wants to share this salvific mission of "restoring" all things to God with all who make themselves available to follow him and to be imbued by the Gospel to the deepest core of their existence. Sharing in the mission of Christ supposes an attitude proper to spouses, that is, to be

totally ready to suffer the same fate, risking everything for him. This participation in the Church's apostolate, in her universal mission, is born from "their spousal love for Christ, (which) becomes in an almost organic way, as it were, love for the Church as the Body of Christ, for the Church as the People of God, for the Church which is at one and the same time Spouse and Mother" (*Redemptionis Donum,* 15).

81. The attitude of spousal association and fidelity to Christ transforms you, then, into an expression of a Church which, like Mary, listens, prays and loves. Like the apostles of all times, you priests, consecrated persons and pastoral workers of Argentina need to live close to Mary in the Upper Room, in order to receive new graces from the Holy Spirit and be able to confront the new situations of evangelization in today's world. This was my invitation in the Encyclical *Dominum et Vivificantem* (cf. nos. 25, 26), as it was also in my first Encyclical *Redemptor Hominis* (cf. n. 22), in the footsteps of the Second Vatican Council (cf. *Lumen Gentium,* 59; *Ad Gentes,* 4). The Marian Year, which will soon begin, gives you an extraordinary occasion to give renewed impulse to your lives according to this evangelical perspective.

82. For your part, the Lord expects you to be able to preach his message with words filled with life, with the transparency of the Gospel itself, because your existence will become an evangelical word to the extent that this word flows spontaneously from your interior gift. Thus, your apostolate will be fruitful and "credible," for the world expects from you a commitment of life and a testimony of prayer, as I desired to show clearly at the meeting in Assisi last year.

83. Preaching the Gospel in this way becomes a "motive for boasting" (cf. 1 Cor 9:16), as Saint Paul tells us in the second reading of this Eucharistic celebration. However, it is precisely because of this fact that the proclamation of the Gospel should seem urgent to us, a holy obligation, as the

same apostle confesses: "Woe to me if I do not preach the Gospel!" (*ibid.*). Yes, woe to me! Woe to us if we do not know how to present the Gospel today to a world which, appearances notwithstanding, continues to have "a hunger for God"! (cf. *Redemptor Hominis,* 18).

84. Thus, beloved brothers and sisters, on this penultimate Friday of Lent, *let us,* therefore, *direct our eyes full of hope* to the Paschal Mystery of the cross and the resurrection of Christ, supreme expression of his redeeming love. The Lord is blessing you with an increase in apostolic vocations, both to the priesthood and the consecrated life. This is his gift; you should be grateful for it and cooperate with it daily. It is necessary to show "the joy of belonging exclusively to God" (*Redemptionis Donum,* 8) both in one's personal life as well as in that of the community. However, that joy, which is an Easter joy, comes from a heart in love with Christ, divested of all the goods of this world, immolated with the Lord on the cross and disposed to share the gift of his love in living with one's brothers and sisters. Many young men and women will feel called to the following of Christ if they see in you the traces of love, the face of Christ who welcomes, helps, reconciles and saves.

85. Live in hope, without letting yourselves be overcome by discouragement, tiredness and criticism. The Lord is with you, because he has chosen you as his instruments that you may bear much fruit and that your fruit will endure (cf. Jn 15:16) in all the areas of the apostolate.

Those of you who are working as "agents of pastoral ministry" will undoubtedly find a concrete area for some evangelizing planning and action, geared towards the renewal of the ecclesial community, in the coming National Catechetical Congress. A well-oriented catechesis is the foundation for sacramental, personal, family and social life, since every apostolic activity and particularly catechesis is "open to the missionary dynamism of the Church" (*Catechesi Tradendae,* 24). I invite all of you to *work together for a continuing evangelization.*

86. Church of Argentina! *"Rise and shine; for your light has come,* and the glory of the Lord has risen above you!" (cf. Is 60:1).

These words of the Prophet Isaiah call to mind the liturgy of the Epiphany or manifestation of the Lord to all the peoples. In this Eucharistic celebration today here in Buenos Aires, the Church is already approaching the Passover of the Lord; the resurrection of Christ is the culminating moment when these words are fulfilled. *The Lord will reveal himself in his mystery of the cross and resurrection.* He will shine with the brightness of the truth to call all peoples with the power of the Spirit: "The peoples shall walk in his light" (Is 60:3).

How I pray to God that Argentina may walk in the light of Christ!

87. Walk with firmness and decision; the Lord takes you by the hand and he will enlighten you with his light so that your foot will not stumble! (cf. Ps 91:12).

When the wealthy consumer societies encounter a serious crisis of spiritual values, your Church, the Church of the entire Latin America, if she remains faithful to Christ, will be able to serve as a light to the world, that it may be able to walk along the path of solidarity, of simplicity, of human and Christian virtues, which are the true foundation of society, of the family, of peace in hearts.

88. Hence, your commitment to evangelization, your mission to be light to enlighten those who are in darkness. You have been called, beloved brothers and sisters, that you may *feel* within you and *live* in all its consequences the *exclamation of Saint Paul,* which becomes the basis of a daily examen: "Woe to me if I do not evangelize!" (1 Cor 9:16).

You have been called and captivated by the example of the love of Christ himself, and also by the example of Saint Paul and of so many holy men and women, apostles and founders, so that you may be weak with the weak, so that you can become "all things to all men in order to save all" (1 Cor 9:22). You have responded to this call for the love of the Gospel, for love of Jesus himself, "in order to have a share in him" (1 Cor 9:23).

89. May your hearts, therefore, overflow with this joy and with the hope announced by the prophet Isaiah and realized in Jesus here and now (cf. Is 60:5).

Praise the Lord in the words of the psalm: "tell among the nations his glory. The Lord reigns" (Ps 95: 3,10). Yes, Christ crucified reigns. By his cross and resurrection Christ is at the center of creation, the Lord of history, redeemer of humanity. He gave us to the Father; he gave us a new life which comes from God and is a participation in the Trinitarian life of donation.

May the most holy Virgin of Lujan become for you the Virgin of the "yes," the Virgin of generous fidelity and of total self-giving to the mission; and may she also be the Virgin of the hope which you have to proclaim and communicate to all your brothers and sisters, making it, first of all, a reality in your own hearts.

Amen.

5

TO WOMEN RELIGIOUS AND A GROUP OF YOUNG WOMEN IN AUGSBURG (GERMANY)

May 4, 1987

90. Let me extend my most cordial greetings to you, the representatives of the various Orders and religious Institutes of the Church in Augsburg. Through you I send my greetings to all your sisters who were not able to be here today—who have duties to attend to in your houses or who are prevented from coming for reasons of age or illness.

I am particularly pleased to see you young Christians here, members of a young women's organization called "The New Road." Through you I send my greetings to all the young people of the diocese of Augsburg who are consciously or unconsciously in search of Jesus Christ and a life fulfilled in him.

Saint Paul wrote in his first epistle to the Corinthians: "The Spirit we have received is not the world's spirit but God's Spirit, *helping us to recognize the gifts he has given us*" (1 Cor 2:12). What gifts has God given us? What opportunities does he open up in our lives?

91. Dear sisters, the opportunity that you have recognized and have come to love is a life in intimate union with Jesus Christ, in which you want to live as he lived himself. His life is your example. His ways of acting are your standards. His Spirit is your strength. Through your union with him you share in his mission in the world and make known the Gospel of God's works of salvation. You find the strength and freedom which your lofty mission exacts from you in a life of celibacy and chastity, undertaken for the Kingdom of heaven; in poverty before God and man; and in obedience to God within a specific community.

92. You have given *your spousal love to the Lord* and have found therein the meaning of your lives. His life, coming from the fullness of the Father, can fulfill each one of your personal lives. Encounters with him in prayer and meditation and a sure faith in his fidelity give you freedom. Thus, you can give yourselves in service to mankind and in the sisterly life of your communities. Have no fear of loss of self or self-denial: God's love embraces you and supports you. This enables you—for the sake of the Kingdom of heaven—to renounce the lofty good of marriage and motherhood. You want to be busy with the Lord's affairs and concerned with pleasing the Lord alone (cf. 1 Cor 7:32).

93. This virginal attitude was realized to perfection in the Virgin Mary. She was busy with the Lord's affairs like no one else, from the Annunciation to her vigil with her Son on the cross. That is why she became the Mother of the entire Church. Many of you bear her name. Carry her example in your hearts and imitate her faithfulness. You light a lamp for the people of our time by showing them that the more a life of continence is led in liberty and dedication, for the sake of the Kingdom of heaven, the more it will lead to joy and fulfillment. Only those who live with their hearts divided, who love half-heartedly, remain in the dark.

94. You, young women, look carefully at this sign of Christian virginity. Do not let yourselves be misled by those who want to bind you to your instincts. Genuine freedom can only be had by those who, through their union with Christ, have found the necessary space to give themselves in the love of God and to his mercy, for the world and its people.

95. Dear sisters, you are living in a country in which many people feel that everything can be bought: possessions, power, recognition and happiness. To many, your *voluntary poverty* may seem scandalous and silly.

However, the human person is more than what he owns. Through your poverty, through your life of simplicity, you are more than what you do, more than what you achieve, more than what you know and perceive. Jesus Christ is your wealth. In this context possessions, power and prestige take on secondary importance. This makes you free. You can let go, be available and be united in solidarity with the "poor" of our times. Through your poverty you have special ties with those who are weak and without rights, those who are exploited and helpless. Place yourselves at their side and stand up for them, with courage and loyalty. Then it can rightfully be said of you: "You are poor but you make others rich; you seem to have nothing, yet everything is yours" (cf. 2 Cor 6:10).

96. As followers of Christ, gladly and consciously accept poverty, as Mary did with Jesus in Bethlehem and Nazareth. In doing so you reflect a prophetic sign of an ultimate and rich life in God.

97. Dear young people, you are in search of the genuine meaning and wealth of your lives. Look at Jesus Christ: he became poor and came into the world in human form for your sake. Your life in God is secure through him. Existential anxieties and insecurity are laid to rest in him. This constitutes your wealth. It is a matter of giving everything to the Lord in order to find everything in him.

Dear sisters, today a great deal is being said about liberation and emancipation, and these preoccupations, justified in themselves, take on a special importance. But is the person who does nothing but shake off commandments and obligations really free? Is such a person able to find his or her way out of the captivity of egoism and hate if he or she views every sort of authority with suspicion?

98. You live lives of *obedience*. You have the freedom of love, since you trust in God and are certain of his love. Your criteria is the obedience of Jesus Christ: "He humbled himself, obediently accepting even death, death

on a cross!" (Phil 2:8). With this basic attitude, you arrive at a mature obedience towards your religious superiors and Church authorities. Your obedience is above all obedience to God; but it must be proven and incarnated in your concrete community and its rule. In your community and along with it you are at the disposition of God; you receive the security and strength you need for the selfless work you carry out. Let yourselves be used as instruments of love.

Here, too, Mary, the Mother of the Lord, is your example. She expressed her "fiat" and in doing so accepted the will of God. Her obedient love led her to the foot of the cross, but also to the joy of the resurrection.

99. Let me ask you one thing, dear young people: don't let yourselves be led astray by false or short-sighted freedom. You are not yet free if you are merely able to do what you feel like doing or what your wallet allows you to do. You are by no means free if you impose your will at the expense of others. Subject your young enthusiasm to the life-giving will of God. Combine your goodwill to form a vigorous community where you can share the same convictions. Engage in a joint search for what is good for you and for others in the long run. It is in this way that you will be free.

100. Dear sisters and young Christians, yours is a very precious vocation—that of being light to the world and witnesses of the Gospel! Don't be faint-hearted. Be courageous! Live with Christ and with his strength, because the Lord assists us in our weakness (cf. Rom 8:26). Give the world testimony of God's friendship for humanity. I wish and pray for all of you that you will achieve increasing perfection in this. God "who has begun the good work in you will carry it through to completion" (cf. Phil 1:6).

For this I extend to you as well as to all your sisters and communities my special apostolic blessing.

Amen.

6

TO THE BROTHERS OF SAINT JOHN OF GOD AND MEMBERS OF THE ORDER OF ST. CAMILLUS

May 7, 1987

101. The occasion for this combined meeting of two religious Orders is truly significant and unique: the commemoration of the first centenary of the proclamation of your founders—Saint Camillus de Lellis and Saint John of God—as patrons of hospitals and of the sick by my predecessor Leo XIII. You have wished to highlight this occasion by coming together in a conference of vast proportions, to discuss the significance and the presence of your two Institutes in today's world and to outline a pastoral program with a view to the future.

For my part, let me first of all express my satisfaction at this initiative so suited to the needs of our times, which require ever greater communion and collaboration among those who have the good fortune to believe in Christ, and all the more so among those who are consecrated to him. I wish to assure you of my keen interest in the problems and concerns related to your Orders' work with the sick and in places of health care.

102. The times in which we have been called to live have brought to light numerous questions which must be faced with serenity and courage, without falling short of the Christian ideals which are the foundation of our life, or the proper charisms of your religious Orders. Pastoral work in hospitals has become more difficult, requiring preparation and special qualities. The reality of volunteer work is certainly a positive one, but one which carries with it a need for evaluation, direction and organization. Relations with the local Churches, with ethical committees, with the pastoral council within the hospital and with

health care workers demand an attentive and constant will to listen and to serve. Above all, great charity, patience and self-giving are required in the effort to humanize places of suffering and to assist those who, in a society of comfort and consumerism, are stricken by illness and the fear of death. In this light I exhort you, dear religious, to open yourselves ever more to your lay collaborators, stimulating in them the desire for a rapport that goes beyond a merely professional scope so as to raise them to the level of participation in your apostolic dimension.

103. I fully understand your pastoral concerns, and I am spiritually close to you—with my esteem, encouragement and prayer—in the hospitals where you serve so many who are ill, especially in the poorest and most needy countries.

Many things have changed, and clearly for the better in many respects, since the time when your saintly founders lived; but the charism of Saint John of God and of Saint Camillus has remained—and must remain—intact in you who are their spiritual sons. That charism saw in every sick person a brother to be loved and served in Christ and like Christ, with the love—as Saint Camillus wrote in the Rule—that a loving mother feels towards her only child who is ill (*Rule, XXVII*) and with the ardor of charity that sprang forth from the heart of Saint John of God and which became concretized in the fourth vow of hospitality.

104. Thanks to the two Orders, founded within a short time of each other, such a concrete and edifying crusade of love for the suffering spread throughout the world that on May 27, 1886, Leo XIII, in the Decree *Inter Omnigenas Virtutes,* declared Saint John of God and Saint Camillus de Lellis patrons of hospitals and of the sick. Later, Pius XI, in the Brief *Expedit Plane* designated them patrons of nurses and nursing associations.

105. Now, after this important European conference, you must continue along your path. In the light of the

example and teachings of your founders, you must be convinced that in order to realize your mission, to humanize hospitals, to serve the sick in today's society, to awaken other vocations to your Orders, what is always and above all necessary is an interior life of depth and conviction. "Apart from me you can do nothing!" (Jn 15:5).

People today have need of your witness as persons who firmly believe and are consecrated to God! Many today tend to reduce Christianity to the sole dimension of love of neighbor, forgetting God, adoration and prayer. Certainly it is important to be sensitive to the civil and charitable responsibilities that Christianity imposes; but one must not forget the first commandment. Jesus gave his life for the redemption of mankind and he was at the same time the first true adorer of the Father.

106. "Technological man," who places all his trust and interest in science and technology for the attainment of maximum well-being, later finds himself disillusioned and embittered before the fatal setbacks of sickness, of moral suffering, of inexorable death. "Technological man" thus becomes a "lonely man," because he feels exhausted, threatened, defeated. Physical pain, together with moral suffering, becomes "existential suffering" and then, in an open or in a hidden way, it becomes "religious suffering," provoking the most profound questions and a search for meaning.

107. The loneliness of modern man and the yearning for an answer that makes existence meaningful are for you a stimulus to ever more ardent and keen pastoral zeal. I appreciate all that you are doing to care for the sick and to humanize hospitals, as well as the effort that animates you in helping the sick and health care workers to acquire or recover with serenity the religious meaning of man's drama. This drama, wrapped as it is in the mystery of Providence, also includes moments of suffering which serve as reminders of the Absolute, and it is necessarily launched towards the transcendent and eternal reality

which lies beyond time and history. The sick have need of experts who provide trust, hope, comfort and support. Together with professional competence, your charism today requires the highest pastoral sensitivity.

108. "Let us not love in word or speech but in deed and in truth," wrote Saint John the apostle (1 Jn 3:18). Many of your confreres heroically gave their lives during the plague and the cholera epidemic, as well as during wartime, while battles raged; they did so precisely because their deep interior lives moved them to such expressions of ardent charity. Now, at the side of the elderly, the marginalized, drug addicts, the sick and the dying, there is just as great a need for love illuminated by Christian faith; there is a need for faith with the human face of kindness.

109. Gazing upon Christ crucified and trusting in Mary, with that ardor of faith exemplified by Saint John of God and Saint Camillus de Lellis, preserve peace in your souls as you bring health and comfort to the sick entrusted to you, as you work together in order to serve better!

May you also be accompanied by my blessing, which I now give you from my heart and extend to your confreres and to the women religious of your Institutes.

7

TO THE INTERNATIONAL UNION OF SUPERIORS GENERAL IN ROME

May 14, 1987

110. It is a great joy for me today to receive such qualified representatives of the consecrated life. You come from many countries, from various cultures, bearing the concerns and the hopes of your sisters and of the peoples among whom your Institutes carry out their apostolate.

The first sentiment that rises in my heart and in the heart of the Church is one of lively gratitude to God. Religious life is, indeed, an integral part of the Church which benefits as a whole from this charism of the consecrated life. Through you, the Church's gratitude reaches all your communities.

Your principal responsibility as superiors general is to assume in the course of daily existence the maternal function of spiritual animation of so many consecrated souls. This is the primordial role of your service. No one can replace you in the accomplishment of this mission which invites you to be attentive and full of affection for the individuals entrusted to you.

111. The more you yourselves are imbued with a filial spirit the better you will be able to fulfill this task. Are you not above all daughters of God, living each day in spiritual joy and in trusting abandonment to the goodness of the heavenly Father? You are also daughters of your founders and foundresses, reflecting in the present situation the characteristic traits of their particular spirituality. You are daughters of your communities which bore you to the religious life and which sustain you daily in your personal sanctification.

You are also sisters, as it were, for our contemporaries whose sufferings and hopes you share. It is your desire to walk with them in the light of the Gospel message. The precise purpose of your meeting in Rome is to do some in-depth study of what forms should be assumed by the prophetic mission of religious life in the Church and in the world.

112. I think it would be opportune to share with you some reflections in relation to the theme of your study on the directives recalled by the Council and repeated on various occasions by my predecessors.

The Gospel should be incarnated in every epoch in concrete situations, in the vicissitudes of peoples and of cultures, while avoiding the snares of possible unilateral or arbitrary theories to which a growth process is always exposed.

Attentive as you are to the needs of our contemporaries, you are very conscious of the evils from which society is suffering in your various countries. In one place, there is extreme poverty, hunger, endemic threats to health; in another, unemployment, the temptation of drugs, the suffering of all categories of the marginalized, and of the newly impoverished. Sometimes a political or economic enslavement, a lack of freedom, and various assaults on the dignity of persons exist. You are rightly sensitive to the dramas that affect the lives of families. It is those in charge of civil society who generally concern themselves with all these things, and many efforts are being made to supply remedies. However, there are other miseries of which you are very aware: moral disorders, the relativism that affects consciences, religious indifference, even unbelief, which are becoming widespread in certain circles.

The ascertaining of these evils, while stimulating the reaction of all believers, finds in your Institutes forces that are more lively, more courageous, more ready to denounce them, to make people aware of them, and above all to help supply effective remedies. The study which you have undertaken, with the help of experts, is aimed at discerning the forms and methods of action most suited to your consecrated state.

113. It is, in fact, your role to enhance and to reinforce the meaning, the dignity and the creative power—which

nothing can replace—of the interior life. The contemplative dimension of the consecrated life should find its vital space in your families of active life, so as to transcend the horizontalism of an apostolate wrongly understood. If the necessary solidarity with one's neighbor does not spring from a contemplative life animated by the love of God, nourished by recollection and participation in the redemptive suffering of Christ, it risks remaining barren, failing to bring to others the salvation they have a right to expect. When a person realizes fully a true vertical relationship with God, as was the case with your founders and foundresses, a new meaning is revealed also in the horizontal relations.

114. In this perspective, the religious makes the option for the poor, not as an exclusive class choice, but as an evangelical option, that is, motivated by the very concern that Christ had for all the poor, which is one of preferential love.

This is why the Church insists that spiritual renewal should always have the primary role, even in the activities of the apostolate (cf. *Perfectae Caritatis,* 2). Recall what the decree *Perfectae Caritatis* says: "The members of each Institute, therefore, ought to seek God before all else, and solely; they should join contemplation, by which they cleave to God by mind and heart, to apostolic love, by which they endeavor to be associated with the work of redemption and to spread the Kingdom of God" (n. 5).

115. Your presence is an eloquent sign of the richness and of the variety of the charisms by which the Holy Spirit enriches the Church, raising up numerous and varied religious families to respond to the multiple demands of the People of God. There is no spiritual or material need towards which your founders and you yourselves are not orientated, according to a wise reading of the signs of the times. Preserve, develop, affirm the choices of the founders! In the urgent needs of the present,

your apostolic service should function concretely according to the specific purpose of your Institute. It could also adopt new forms which would be compatible with the founder's charism, in line with the most sure and sound tradition, in harmony with the intentions the Church had in approving your Institutes.

116. It would be a somewhat equivocal zeal which would lead you to occupy the apostolic field of another under the pretext of exceptional needs. Today one sometimes encounters a prejudice according to which one should contemptuously ignore the "differences" which constitute and distinguish the religious Institutes from one another. Each Institute should be careful to maintain its own nature, the special character of its own *raison d'être* which has exercised an attraction, has stimulated vocations, particular aptitudes, and has given a noteworthy public witness. It is naive and presumptuous to believe that, in the last analysis, each Institute should be identical to all the others in practicing a general love of God and of neighbor. To think thus would be to neglect an essential aspect of the Mystical Body: the heterogeneity of its constitution, the pluralism of models in which is revealed the vitality of the Spirit who animates it, the transcendent human and divine perfection of Christ, its Head, who can be imitated only by the manifold resources of the human soul animated by grace (cf. *Perfectae Caritatis*, 2b).

117. Regarding the specific theme which has been the object of your study during these days, I think it is useful once again to underline the importance of supernatural charity which is the specific characteristic of Christians.

The social history of the Church has always been rich in accomplishments. The Church has protected infants, educated the young; she has assisted the sick, the elderly, the refugees, the imprisoned, defending the rights of the most humble categories against every form of oppression and of exploitation.

Yet the justice which she has promoted has always been animated by the love of Christ. The Word became flesh above all to redeem the world from sin, the worst of all injustices. He founded the Church above all to save human beings by making them beneficiaries of his redemptive passion.

In this theological perspective, the secret of a truly prophetic life resides in the existential consistency of the religious woman with the witness which she gives. She is not content with taking up in turn the contestation and the condemnation of injustices. Rather, she offers her own life as a humble and silent message, animated by the purest and certainly effective love.

118. It pertains to religious, both men and women, to be in the world "what the soul is for the body," as the epistle to Diognetus said of the first Christians (cf. *Lumen Gentium,* 38). They must live like pilgrims in the midst of corruption, in expectation of the incorruption of heaven. Their pilgrimage is, as it were, an incessant proclamation of the Kingdom in process of realization, because he who has conquered the world has promised it.

In this way, religious profession can achieve a prophetic role, which, in the very works of social service carried to the point of heroism, cannot be compared to activity that remains circumscribed in an inevitably ephemeral present.

The consecrated person should be a banner of hope raised over this world: the hope of a better, purified, renewed world, transparent to the light and love of God, as we expect it to be in the world which is to come, but possible and inaugurated already today.

119. In the fulfillment of your apostolic mission, you have for a model the figure of Mary, to whom we have decided to dedicate a year at the approach of the third millennium.

In her hymn of praise to God, the *Magnificat,* one finds echoes of the prophetic tradition of the Chosen People.

This canticle reflects the interior world of the Virgin of Nazareth. It reveals not only the secret of her relationship with God—marked by full confidence and filial gratitude—but also her attitude towards the world of humanity where the humble, the poor and the simple are exalted.

I hope, together with you, that all your sisters are able to look on Mary in this way. May they discover ever more deeply in her the model of their consecration to God, and at the same time that of their apostolic engagement in the service of their neighbors. While praying that the Holy Spirit will animate your lives as he did Mary's, I wholeheartedly impart to you and to your religious families a special blessing.

8

TO CLOISTERED RELIGIOUS IN WARSAW

June 8, 1987

120. I wish to express my deep joy at the fact that the *first meeting* on the program of my third pilgrimage to my homeland *is with you, cloistered sisters.*

You have assembled in the Cathedral of Saint John in Warsaw, where I come to meet *the Church of the archdiocese that includes the capital.* I also come to kneel *at the tomb of the late Primate of the Millennium,* where many fellow countrymen come to pray. Certainly this is often *a prayer for our homeland* since it is the place where he who "so loved the Church of Christ" lies; he who so faithfully loved the homeland and every person, defending his dignity and his rights, pardoning enemies, "overcoming evil with good" (cf. Rom 12:21). A man *"of heroic faith" who "placed all his confidence in Mary and entrusted himself to her without limits...he turned to her for help in defending the faith of Christ and the liberty of the nation."*

It is with these words that the Church on Polish soil prays at the tomb of the late Primate, and I too repeat this prayer.

121. I believe the Primate of the Millennium is rejoicing because, through the initiative of his successor and of the entire episcopate, *the second national Eucharistic Congress* is being held in Poland after fifty years. Particularly because it finds its theme in these words of Christ, taken from the Gospel of John: *"having loved his own...he loved them to the end"* (Jn 13:1). In fact, for his whole life and during his pastoral service, the late Primate sought to manifest his own fidelity to such a love: "to the end." In it *is expressed the particular fullness of the Gospel,* its particular "evangelical radicalness," one might say.

122. This is also your portion, dear Sisters. *This is your vocation*. You have chosen Christ as your one Spouse, aware of this love of his "to the end." Indeed, *you have chosen this love* as your ideal, as the purpose of your cloistered vocation. Following Christ's example, you too wish "to love to the end." Your brothers and sisters in the world know this. When they come often to ask your prayers, they also come to receive words of encouragement, to receive the light that radiates from your silence in God. It is difficult not to mention this as well: that when the need presented itself—as, for example, during the years of the occupation, and especially during the Warsaw Insurrection—the nuns of cloistered convents showed themselves ready to serve their brothers and sisters (the wounded, the homeless, the hunted), ready to make this sacrifice, which was accepted by God. I recall the case of the Warsaw convent of the Sacramentine Sisters, in the New City, and many others. In this way they "loved to the end."

123. Your vocation is inscribed in all the Gospel as *a particular counsel of our Master*. He does not ask it of everyone. He does not require of everyone the *poverty, chastity and obedience* to which you bind yourselves through your vows. "He who is able to receive this, let him receive it!" (Mt 19:12), says the Master after having presented to his disciples the ideal "of celibacy for the Kingdom of God" (cf. *ibid.*). Not only this passage, however, but the whole Gospel opens before us a vision of life according to the living example of Jesus of Nazareth, of a life of which *the eight Beatitudes* remain a particular synthesis.

124. Dear sisters! How ardently I rejoice that the Church in Poland is gifted with the witness of your vocation. Today, on the threshold of the Eucharistic Congress, I wish to say that this vocation is in special *harmony with the essential theme of this Congress:* "he loved to the end." Thus it is not by chance that my first meeting is with you.

In fact, you carry throughout your daily life the truth of Christ expressed in these words.

125. *Your life* in the cloister—contemplative, spousal, sacrificial—*is born of the Eucharist in a special way.* And it also *leads to the Eucharist* in a special way, it proclaims it—even though you live a hidden life. Your whole life proclaims the Eucharist—the sacrament of Christ's love "to the end"—through the walls of your convents and the grilles of your cloisters.

"To live the life of the Eucharist is to exit completely from the small circle of one's own life and to grow in the infinity of the life of Christ." These are the words of Blessed Teresa Benedicta of the Cross, a Carmelite whom I beatified a short time ago (Edith Stein, *Autobiography,* translationofSr. Immakulata Adamsda OCD, in *"Swiatlosc w ciemnosci,"* Vol. I, Krakow, 1977, p. 243).

126. Through the Eucharist you find yourselves every day in the very "heart" of your vocation. You find yourselves in the "heart" of the Church, as the holy Carmelite of Lisieux wrote. The heart of the Church, in fact, *beats with the rhythm of the Eucharist.* This is the rhythm of the love with which Christ *"having loved his own...loved them to the end."* Thus this love continues, embraced by many, many human hearts, embraced in a particular way by your hearts, dear sisters.

This love will continue to the end of time, so that—beyond the bounds of time—*it may manifest itself in all its fullness. In its truly divine fullness.* For this reason love is "the greatest" (cf. 1 Cor 13:13).

127. "...Thus, even though the many different apostolic works... are extremely important, nevertheless the truly fundamental work of the apostolate remains always *what* (and at the same time *who*) *you are* in the Church. Of each of you can be repeated, with special appropriateness, these words of Saint Paul: 'For you have died, and your life is hidden with Christ in God' (Col 3:3)" (*Redemptionis*

Donum, 15).

You, my dear sisters, are only apparently separated from the world. In reality, you find yourselves *at its very center*—at the center of temporal reality—at the center of the reality of Poland—through *the mystery of the Church.* You know well that this reality is difficult, full of painful tensions, full of uncertainties and of human crises, *aggravated by sin,* which, at times, is the consequence of human weakness, but not always....

128. Within the cloister, *one is not concerned with questions of personal status.* Within the cloister, *one loves.* With the love with which Christ loved "to the end." This love is the Gospel "leaven"; *it is the leaven* which "leavens all the dough" (cf. Mt 13:33) in the bread necessary for man's daily, mortal life.

Like *the Eucharist—the bread of immortality.*

My hope is that you may be precisely this "leaven."

9

TO THE GENERAL CHAPTER OF THE MONTFORT MISSIONARIES

July 20, 1987

Receiving the members of the General Chapter at his residence in Castel Gandolfo, the Holy Father spontaneously addressed them in French, as follows:

129. Thank you for your visit, on this memorable day when the Church, and in particular, the Holy See and the Church of Rome, celebrate with you the fortieth anniversary of the canonization of your illustrious founder, Saint Louis-Marie Grignoin de Montfort, with the liturgy that we celebrated this morning. He is a great figure in the history of the Church and, above all, in the history of the Marian spirituality of the Church. This spirituality is profoundly linked to the central mysteries of our faith, above all to the mystery of the Most Holy Trinity and to the mysteries of the Incarnation and the redemption.

It is through these mysteries that Saint Louis-Marie taught us to know the Virgin Mary. One could even say that he "inverted" the paths, or that he gave the paths a new complementarity, because traditionally, it was thought that one went *to Jesus through Mary;* he taught us to go to her *through Jesus,* in these mysteries (the mysteries of the Trinity, the Incarnation, the redemption).

130. Of course, these two movements of our spiritual journey complete one another. It is invaluable to understand this Marian spirituality of Saint Louis-Marie Grignoin de Montfort. It is invaluable to be able to say with him, as you have sung this morning: "Totus tuus ego sum et omnia mea tua sunt; accipio te in mea omnia...et ego sum servus Mariae." (I am all yours and all that I have

is yours; I take you into all that is mine...and I am the slave of Mary). It is a true résumé of Marian spirituality, as we find it in the Gospel itself. "Accipio te in mea omnia"; it was the apostle John who received the Virgin Mary in this way, beneath the cross of Jesus on Calvary.

131. You have stressed that the two orientations, the missionary and the Marian orientations, go together. This is characteristic of and specific to your Congregation, which takes its inspiration from Saint Louis-Marie Grignoin de Montfort. It is true, and I would even say that it was particularly emphasized in the encyclical "Redemptoris Mater." And also, above all, in the doctrine of Vatican II in Lumen Gentium, Chapter VIII, which is the Marian chapter of Lumen Gentium: "The Role of the Blessed Virgin Mary, Mother of God, in the Mystery of Christ and the Church."

...Mary is present in these mysteries as she who precedes, who precedes through faith, who precedes the entire People of God. When we say that "she precedes," it is not only in the sense of her dignity; we say that she "precedes" above all because of her activity, her "mission." She is still on a mission; she has been on mission since the Incarnation, but even more so since the redemption, since the moment on Calvary when she was sent in a special manner, not by a formal mandate, but by the force of these words: "Behold your son...behold your Mother...".

Since that moment, she has become an expression of the Church, of that Church which is missionary by its very nature. "She precedes": that means that she always places herself at the heart of the Church's mission, a salvific mission, a redemptive mission, as a missionary of evangelization. She is always found in the midst of, at the center of, at the heart of this Church which is on mission.

132. Your missionary Congregation, which is, at the same time, of a profoundly Marian inspiration, gives a very specific expression to the spirituality of Saint Louis-Marie, to that spirituality which also emanates from

Vatican II and of which my last encyclical, "Redemptoris Mater," is intended to be only a little commentary.

And so, I wish you, on this occasion, the spiritual success which is proper to those who have left all to serve the Lord and who do it in a spirit of total confidence in the Virgin Mary, Mother of the Lord, in that spirit which your founder promoted so much, and above all, which he lived.

10

TO SEMINARIANS AND CANDIDATES FOR THE RELIGIOUS LIFE IN SAN ANTONIO, TEXAS

September 13, 1987

133. "Remove the sandals from your feet, for *the place where you stand is holy ground*" (Ex 3:5). These words of God marked the beginning of a new way of life for Moses. The place where he was standing was holy ground, for he was standing in *the awesome presence of Almighty God.* And on that holy ground, he heard a voice calling him to a special mission of service to the People of God. From that moment forward, Moses' life would be radically altered. He would henceforth place his life at the service of the God of Abraham, Isaac and Jacob. No longer would his life be his own. He would lead the Chosen People out of slavery in Egypt towards freedom in the Promised Land. In meeting God on holy ground, speaking with him there, and hearing his summons to service, Moses came to a new understanding of himself and entered into a deeper commitment to God and his people. *The mission of Moses began under the sign of God's holiness.*

134. Dear brothers and sisters in the Lord: it is a deep joy for me to be with you today in this historic *Cathedral of San Fernando,* the oldest cathedral sanctuary in the United States. It is with great gratitude to God that I meet you who are preparing to serve the Lord as priests and religious, you who in a singular and remarkable way have, like Moses, heard the voice of God calling you to *that "holy ground" of a special vocation in the Church.* You have stood in the awesome presence of the Lord and heard him call you by name. And listening to his voice with prayerful discernment, you have joyfully begun your formation for the priesthood or the religious life.

135. A vocation in the Church, from the human point of view, *begins with a discovery,* with finding the pearl of great price. You discover Jesus: his person, his message, his call. In the Gospel which we have heard today, we reflect on the call of Jesus to the first disciples. The first thing that Andrew did after meeting Jesus was to seek out his brother Simon and tell him: *"We have found the Messiah!"* Then Philip, in a similar way, sought out Nathanael and told him: "*We have found* the one Moses spoke of in the Law—the prophets too—*Jesus,* son of Joseph, from Nazareth" (cf. Jn 1:35-51).

136. After the initial discovery, a dialogue in prayer ensues, a dialogue between Jesus and the one called, *a dialogue which goes beyond words* and expresses itself in love.

Questions are an important part of this dialogue. For example, in the Gospel account of the call of the disciples, we are told that "when Jesus turned around and noticed them following him, he asked them, *'What are you looking for?'* They said to him, 'Rabbi' (which means teacher), 'where do you stay?' *'Come and see,'* he answered" (Jn 1:38-39).

What begins as a discovery of Jesus moves to a greater understanding and commitment through *a prayerful process of questions and discernment.* In this process, our motives are purified. We come face to face with pointed questions such as "What are you looking for?" And we even find ourselves asking questions of Jesus, as Nathanael did: *"How do you know me?"* (Jn 1:48). It is only when we have reflected candidly and honestly in the silence of our hearts that we begin to be convinced that the Lord is truly calling us.

137. Yet, even then, the process of discernment is not over. Jesus says to us as he said to Nathanael: *"You will see much greater things than that"* (Jn 1:50). Throughout our lives, after we have made a sacred and permanent commitment and after our active service of the

Lord has begun, we still need the dialogue of prayer that will continually deepen our knowledge and love of our Lord Jesus Christ.

Dear students for the priesthood and candidates for the religious life: you stand in *a long line of people who have given themselves totally* for the sake of the Kingdom of God, and who have shared our Lord's Sacrifice and entered into his Paschal victory. For generations many of the generous priests and religious who have served the Church in Texas have come with immigrants from other lands, or as missionaries from other places. I wish to express my gratitude to God for the contribution which they have made to establishing the Church here. At the same time I praise the Lord of the harvest for all of you and for the growing number of native born vocations, and I fervently pray that this increase continues.

138. Like all those who have gone before you, you will have trials. Your fidelity will be ensured only when you invoke the strength of the Lord, only when you rely on Christ's grace. But if Christ is the center of your lives, the one for whom you live and die, then your generous service to your brothers and sisters will know no limits. You will love those who are difficult to love, and you will *enrich the world with the Gospel* of Jesus Christ.

I would now like to speak *to the seminarians.* Dear brothers in Christ: as men preparing for priestly ordination, it is important for you to have *a clear understanding of the vocation* to which you feel called so that your promise of lifelong fidelity may be maturely made and faithfully kept. Your life in the priesthood will closely join you with the Eucharist; you will be ministers of the mysteries of God; you will be expected to preach and teach in the name of the Church.

139. *The Eucharist is the principal reason for the ordained priesthood.* As I said in my 1980 Holy Thursday Letter: "Through our ordination...we priests are united in a singular and exceptional way to the Eucharist. In a

certain way we derive *from* it and exist *for it*" (n. 2). No work we do as priests is so important. The celebration of the Eucharist is the way that we best serve our brothers and sisters in the world because it is the source and center of the dynamism of their Christian lives.

140. How crucial it is then, for our own happiness and for the sake of a fruitful ministry, that we *cultivate a deep love for the Eucharist*. During your seminary days, a thorough theological study of the nature of the Eucharistic mystery and an accurate knowledge of liturgical norms will prepare you well to foster the full, conscious and active participation of the community in the liturgy. The future priest is called to reflect and to profess with the Second Vatican Council that "the other sacraments, as well as every ministry of the Church and every work of the apostolate, are linked with the Holy Eucharist and are directed towards it. For the most Blessed Eucharist contains the Church's entire spiritual wealth, that is, Christ himself" (*Presbyterorum Ordinis,* 5).

141. The task of *preaching the Gospel* is of supreme importance in the priesthood. And since, as Saint Paul says, "faith comes through hearing, and what is heard is the word of Christ" (Rom 10:17), seminary formation must aim at fostering *a deep understanding of the Word of God* as it is lived and proclaimed by the Church. Always remember the words of the prophet Jeremiah: "When I found your words, I devoured them; they became my joy and the happiness of my heart, because I bore your name, O Lord" (Jer 15:16).

In order for your preaching to bear fruit in the lives of those whom you will serve, you will have to nourish in your own mind and heart *a real internal adherence to the Magisterium* of the Church. For, as the Council reminded us, "the task of priests is not to teach their own wisdom but God's Word, and to summon all people urgently to conversion and to holiness" (*Presbyterorum Ordinis,* 4).

142. The priest needs to know the real living conditions of the people he serves, and he must live among them as a true brother in Christ. He can never be separated from the community. But there is a real sense in which, like the apostle Paul, he is, in the very words of Scripture, *"set apart to proclaim the Gospel of God"* (Rom 1:1). In his priestly identity he is commissioned for a special service, a unique service, to the Body of Christ. For this reason, the Second Vatican Council spoke in this way: "By their vocation and ordination, priests of the New Testament are indeed set apart in a certain sense within the midst of God's people. But this is so, not that they may be separated from this people or from any man, but that they may be totally dedicated to the work for which the Lord raised them up. They cannot be ministers of Christ unless they are witnesses and dispensers of a life other than this earthly one" (*ibid.,* 3).

143. Each one of you is called to embrace freely a celibate life for the sake of Jesus and his Kingdom, in order to become a "man for others." If modeled on the generous divine and human love of Jesus for his Father and for every man, woman and child, your celibacy will mean an enhancement of your life, *a greater closeness to God's people,* an eagerness to give yourself without reserve. By embracing celibacy in the context of the priesthood, you are committing yourself to a deeper and more universal love. Above all *celibacy means the gift of yourself to God.* It will be the response, in Christ and the Church, to the gifts of creation and redemption. It will be part of your sharing, at the deepest level of human freedom and generosity, in the death and resurrection of Jesus. Humanly speaking this sacrifice is difficult because of our human weaknesses; without prayer it is impossible. It will also require discipline and effort and persevering love on your part. But in your gift of celibacy to Christ and his Church, even the world will be able to see the meaning of the Lord's grace and the power of his Paschal Mystery. This victory must always be visible in your joy.

144. The Council stressed the *essential difference* between the ordained priesthood and the priesthood of all the baptized, and prescribed a priestly formation in seminaries which is distinct from other forms of formation (cf. *Lumen Gentium,* 10; *Optatam Totius,* 4). At the heart of this essential difference is the truth that Jesus entrusted the Twelve with the authority to proclaim the Gospel, celebrate the Eucharist, forgive sins and provide for the pastoral care of the community. This authority is given for a truly specific purpose and through ordination is shared by the successors of the apostles and their collaborators in the ordained priesthood. It is given for *a particular ministry of service* to be carried out in imitation of the Son of Man who came to serve. The ministry of the ordained priest is essential to the life and development of the Church; it is an essential service to the rest of the Church. It is clear that those who are preparing for this specific ministry will have *special needs and requirements* that differ from those of the rest of the community.

145. All the members of the Church are summoned to share in her mission by reason of their baptism and confirmation. Priests can best assist and encourage others in the service of the Gospel by being faithful themselves to their priestly ministry in the Church. "Hence, whether engaged in prayer and adoration, preaching the word, offering the Eucharistic Sacrifice, and ministering the other sacraments, or performing any of the works of the ministry for people, priests are contributing to the extension of God's glory as well as to the development of divine life in people" (*Presbyterorum Ordinis,* 2).

146. And now I turn to you, my brothers and sisters who are preparing for the *religious life.* Yours too is a great and specific gift of God's love. To each of you, as to the first disciples, Jesus has said: *"Come and see"* (Jn 1:39). There is no force or coercion on the part of Christ, but rather an invitation, extended simply and personally, to come and stay in his house, to be in his presence, and with him to praise his Father in the unity of the Holy Spirit.

147. A religious vocation is *a gift,* freely given and freely received. It is a profound expression of *the love of God* for you and, on your part, it requires in turn *a total love for Christ.* Thus, the whole life of a religious is aimed at strengthening the bond of love which was first forged in the *sacrament of Baptism.* You are called to do this in religious consecration through the profession of the evangelical counsels of chastity, poverty and obedience (cf. can. 573, par. 1-2).

148. During your years of preparation, the Church is eager that you receive a formation that will prepare you to live your religious consecration in fidelity and joy, a formation that is both deeply human and Christian, a formation that will help you to accept ever more generously *the radical demands of the Gospel* and bear public witness to them. Your very life is meant to be a confident and convincing affirmation that Jesus is "the Way, and the Truth, and the Life" (Jn 14:6).

149. What you must develop, first and foremost, is *the habit and discipline of prayer.* For who you *are* is more fundamental than any service you perform. In this regard, the Second Vatican Council said that religious should "seek God before all things" and "combine contemplation with apostolic love" (*Perfectae Caritatis,* 5). This is no easy task, for prayer has many dimensions and forms. It is both personal and communal, liturgical and private. It deepens our union with God and fosters our apostolic love. A climate of silence is needed as well as a personal lifestyle that is simple and ready for sacrifice.

150. The liturgical life of the community greatly influences the personal prayer of all the members. The *Eucharist* will always be the source and summit of your life in Christ. It is the sacrament through which *the worship of your whole existence is presented to God in union with Christ* (cf. can. 607, par. 1). The Eucharist is the point where the offering of your chastity, poverty and obedience is made one with the sacrifice of Christ.

151. In your religious consecration, *the sacrament of Penance* is a constant reminder to you of the call of Jesus to conversion and newness of life. Precisely because you are called by your religious profession to bear witness to the holiness of God, you must help the People of God *never to lose their sense of sin.* To be authentic in following Christ in the perfection of charity, you must be the first to recognize sin in your hearts, to repent and to glorify God's grace and mercy. Conversion is a lifelong process requiring repentant love. The sacrament of Penance is the sacrament in which our weakness meets God's holiness in the mercy of Christ.

152. In a thousand ways the Church will call you into service in her mission for the Kingdom of God. She needs your talents, your availability to come and go according to the needs of the hour, which are often the needs of the poor. She needs your collaboration in the cause of faith and justice. *She needs your work* and everything that you can do for the Gospel. But, above all, the Church needs what you are; *she needs you:* men and women consecrated to God, living in union with Christ, living in union with his Church, striving after the perfection of love. Why? *Because of the holiness of God!* Dear brothers and sisters: *what you do is important, but what you are is even more important*—more important for the world, more important for the Church, more important for Christ.

153. In Mary, the Mother of Christ and the Church, you will understand the identity of your own life. She showed throughout her life the meaning of the evangelical counsels, to which your religious consecration is directed. Her words to the angel—"I am the servant of the Lord. Let it be done to me as you say" (Lk 1:38)—show the obedient total surrender which our consecration to God requires and which your vows express.

154. Of course, *the call to holiness* is a *universal* call. All members of the Church, without exception, are sum-

moned by God to grow in personal sanctity and to share in the mission of the Church. A heightened awareness of this truth has been one of the fruits of the Second Vatican Council. And it has helped foster a clearer awareness of *the role of the laity* in building up the Kingdom, as well as a closer collaboration of the laity with the clergy and religious. As persons preparing for the priesthood and religious life, it will be your privilege to help explore still more effective forms of collaboration in the future. But even more importantly, you will be in a position to encourage the lay people to fulfill *that mission which is uniquely their own* in those situations and places in which the Church can be the salt of the earth only through them.

155. The Council spoke very clearly about their special mission. Among other things it stated: "The laity, by their very vocation, seek the Kingdom of God by engaging in temporal affairs and by ordering them according to the plan of God. They live in the world, that is, in each and in all of the secular professions and occupations. They live in the ordinary circumstances of family and social life, from which the very web of their existence is woven" (*Lumen Gentium,* 31). This activity of the laity constitutes a specific contribution to the Body of Christ. Yours is another charism, a different gift to be lived differently, so that, *in true diversity,* there may be real unity in the work of service.

156. On this occasion, I cannot fail to express my special gratitude and encouragement to those of you who are responsible for the formation of candidates for the priesthood and religious life. Be assured that all your efforts, work and sacrifice are deeply appreciated by the Church and by me personally. Your task is a vital one for the future of the Church, and your contribution to the life of the People of God is a lasting one. Certainly it is crucial that you yourselves be steeped in sound doctrine, pastoral experience and holiness of life. Of great importance is your attitude of faith, and particularly your personal example

of *filial love for the Church,* as well as *your loyal adherence to her authentic ordinary Magisterium* (cf. *Lumen Gentium,* 25). Saint Paul tells us: "Christ loved the Church. He gave himself up for her to make her holy" (Eph 5:25-26). I pray that your own lives will be always animated by this kind of sacrificial love.

157. I wish to add a word of deep appreciation to all those parents who sustain and encourage their children in the following of Christ. The prayerful support, understanding and love that you give them is of immense value.

At this time I wish to appeal to the Church in the United States for *vocations* to the priesthood and religious life. The duty of fostering such vocations rests on the whole Christian community, and certainly families have traditionally made the greatest contribution. We must always remember too the impact on vocations that can be made by zealous priests and religious, by their example of generous service, by the witness of their charity, their goodness and their joy. Above all, *the key to vocations is persevering prayer,* as Jesus himself commanded: "The harvest is good but laborers are scarce. Beg the harvest master to send out laborers to gather his harvest" (Mt 9:37-38).

158. Dear brothers and sisters: you have come to know the Lord Jesus. You have *heard his voice, discovered his love, and answered his call.* May he, the Lord Jesus, who has begun this good work in you bring it to completion for the glory of his Father and by the power of his Spirit. Remember always: "the place where you stand is holy ground" (Ex 3:5). And may the Blessed Virgin Mary help you by her prayers, and by the example of her love.

11

TO MEN AND WOMEN RELIGIOUS IN SAN FRANCISCO

September 17, 1987

159. In their deepest spiritual significance, the Vespers that we are praying together are *the voice of the Bride* addressing the Bridegroom (cf. *Sacrosanctum Concilium,* 84). They are also *the voice of the Bridegroom,* "the very prayer which Christ himself, together with his Body, addresses to the Father" (*ibid.*). With one and the same voice the Bride and the Bridegroom praise the Father in the unity of the Holy Spirit.

In this liturgical song of praise we give expression to "the real nature of the true Church"—"both human and divine, visible and yet invisibly endowed, eager to act and yet devoted to contemplation, present in the world and yet not at home in it" (*ibid.,* 2). It is precisely *the presence of God* in human life and human affairs that you proclaim through your religious consecration and the practice of the evangelical counsels. It is to the reality of *God's love in the world* that you bear witness by means of the many forms of your loving service to God's people.

160. Dear religious sisters, and religious priests and brothers: for me, this is one of the most important moments of my visit. Here, with all of you, men and women religious of the United States, and in the spiritual presence of all the members of your Congregations spread throughout this land or serving in other countries, *I give heartfelt thanks to God for each and every one of you.* He who is mighty has done great things for you, holy is his name! (cf. Lk 1:49).

I greet each one of you with love and gratitude. I thank you for the warm welcome you have given me and I thank Sister Helen Garvey and Father Stephen Tutas, who have presented a picture of your dedicated lives. I rejoice because of your deep love of the Church and your generous service to God's people. Every place I have visited in this vast country bears the marks of the diligent labor and immense spiritual energies of religious of both contemplative and active Congregations in the Church. The extensive Catholic educational and health care systems, the highly developed network of social services in the Church—none of this would exist today, were it not for your highly motivated dedication and the dedication of those who have gone before you. The spiritual vigor of so many Catholic people testifies to the efforts of generations of religious in this land. The history of the Church in this country is in large measure *your history at the service of God's people.*

161. As we remember your glorious past, let us be filled with hope that *your future* will be no less beneficial for the Church in the United States, and no less a prophetic witness of God's Kingdom to each new generation of Americans.

The single most extraordinary event that has affected the Church in every aspect of her life and mission during the second half of the twentieth century has been the Second Vatican Council. The Council called the whole Church to conversion, to "newness of life," to renewal—to a *renewal that consists essentially in an ever increasing fidelity to Jesus Christ her divine Founder.* As "men and women who more closely follow and more clearly demonstrate the Savior's self-giving" (*Lumen Gentium,* 42), it is only natural that religious should have experienced the call to renewal in a radical way.

162. Thousands of religious in the United States have generously responded to this call, and continue to live it, with profound commitment. The results, the good fruits of this response are evident in the Church: we see a Gospel-inspired spirituality, which has led to a deepening of personal and liturgical prayer; a clearer sense of the

Church as a communion of faith and love in which the grace and responsibility entrusted to each member are to be respected and encouraged; a new appreciation of the legacy of your founders and foundresses, so that the specific charism of each Congregation stands out more clearly; a heightened awareness of the urgent needs of the modern world where religious, in close union with the bishops and in close collaboration with the whole Church, seek to carry on the work of the Good Shepherd, the Good Samaritan and the Good Teacher.

163. It would be unrealistic to think that such a deep and overall process of renewal could take place without risks and errors, without undue impatience on the part of some and undue fears on the part of others. Whatever the tension and polarization occasioned by change, whatever the mistakes made in the past, I am sure that all of you are convinced that the time has come *to reach out once again to one another in a spirit of love and reconciliation,* both within and beyond your Congregations.

During the past two decades, there have also been profound insights into the meaning and value of religious life. Many of these insights, conceived in the experience of prayer and penance and authenticated by the teaching charism of the Church, have contributed greatly to ecclesial life. These insights have borne witness to *the enduring identity of religious consecration and mission* in the life of the Church. At the same time they have testified to the need for religious to adapt their activity to the needs of the people of our times.

164. Fundamental to the Council's teaching on religious life is an emphasis on *the ecclesial nature of the vocation to observe the evangelical counsels.* Religious consecration "belongs inseparably to the life and holiness of the Church" (*Lumen Gentium,* 44). "The counsels are a divine gift, which the Church has received from her Lord and which she ever preserves with the help of his grace" (*ibid.,* 43). It was precisely within this ecclesial context

that in 1983 I asked the bishops of the United States to render a pastoral service by offering to those of you whose Institutes are engaged in apostolic works special encouragement and support in living your ecclesial vocation to the full. I now wish to thank the bishops and all of you for your very generous collaboration in this important endeavor. In particular I thank the Pontifical Commission headed by Archbishop John Quinn. By God's grace there now exists a fresh cooperative spirit between your religious Institutes and the local Churches.

165. *Your continuing participation in the mission of the Church at the diocesan and parish levels is of inestimable value* to the well-being of the local Churches. Your communion with the local bishops and collaboration with the pastoral ministry of the diocesan clergy contributes to a strong and effective spiritual growth among the faithful. Your creative initiatives in favor of the poor and all marginalized persons and groups, whose needs might otherwise be neglected, are deeply appreciated. Your evangelizing and missionary work both at home and in other parts of the world is one of the great strengths of the Church in the United States. Alongside your traditional apostolates—which are as important now as ever before and which I encourage you to appreciate in their full significance—you are engaged in almost every area of defending human rights and of building a more just and equitable society. This is *a record of unselfish response to the Gospel of Jesus Christ.* Yes, the entire Church in the United States benefits from the dedication of American religious to their ecclesial mission.

166. At the same time you are concerned about certain weaknesses affecting the structure of your Institutes. The decline in vocations and the aging of your membership are serious challenges for each one of your Institutes and for the corporate reality of religious life, and yet these are not new phenomena in the long experience of the Church. History teaches us that in ways generally unpredictable

the radical "newness" of the Gospel message is always able to inspire successive generations to do what you have done, to renounce all for the sake of the Kingdom of God, in order to possess the pearl of great price (cf. Mt 13:44-45).

167. You are called at this hour to fresh courage and trust. Your *joyful witness to consecrated love*—in chastity, poverty and obedience—will be the greatest human attraction for young people to religious life in the future. When they sense the authenticity of renewal in you and your communities, they too will be disposed to come and see! The invitation is directly from Christ but they will want to hear it from you too. Your own essential contribution to vocations will come *through fidelity, penance and prayer,* and through confidence in *the power of Christ's Paschal Mystery to make all things new.*

In the best traditions of Christian love, you will know how to show your special appreciation for the aged and infirm members of your communities, whose contribution of prayer and penance, suffering and faithful love is of immense value to your apostolates. May they always be comforted in knowing that they are respected and loved within their own religious families.

168. Your vocation is, of its very nature, a radical response to the call which Jesus extends to all believers in their baptismal consecration: *"Seek first his kingship over you, his way of holiness"* (Mt 6:33). Your response is expressed by your vowed commitment to embrace and live in community the evangelical counsels. Through chastity, poverty and obedience you live in expectation of an eschatological kingdom where "they neither marry nor are given in marriage" (Mt 22:30). And so, even now, "where your treasure is there your heart is also" (Mt 6:21).

169. Through your religious profession, the consecration which the Holy Spirit worked in you at baptism is *powerfully directed anew to the perfection of charity.* By

practicing the vows, you constantly die with Christ in order to rise to new life with him (cf. Rom 6:8). In fidelity to your vow of *chastity* you are empowered to love with the love of Christ and to know that deep encounter with his love which inspires and sustains your apostolic love for your neighbor. Treading the path of *poverty* you find yourselves truly open to God and aligned with the poor and suffering in whom you see the image of the poor and suffering Christ (cf. Mt 25:31 ff.). And through *obedience* you are intimately united with Jesus in seeking always to fulfill the Father's will. Through such obedience there is unlocked in you *the full measure of Christian freedom* which enables you to serve God's people with selfless and unfailing devotion. The Catholic people, and indeed the vast majority of your fellow citizens, have the highest respect for your religious consecration and they look to you for the "proof" of the transcendent Christian hope that is in you (cf. 1 Pt 3:15).

170. The disciple, though, is not above the Master. It is only right for you to expect, as has always been the Church's understanding, that if you follow the laws of Christ's Kingdom—in essence, the new commandment of love and the new values proclaimed in the Beatitudes—you will be *in conflict with the "wisdom of this age"* (cf. 1 Cor 2:6). In a particularly personal and courageous way, religious have always been in the front line of this never ending struggle.

Today, the encounter between the saving message of the Gospel and the forces that shape our human culture calls for *a profound and prayerful discernment* of Christ's will for his Church at this moment of her life. In this regard the Second Vatican Council remains the necessary point of reference and the guiding light. This discernment is the work of the whole Church. No person or group of people can claim to possess sufficient insights so as to monopolize it. All members of the Church, according to the ministry received for the good of the whole Body, must be humbly attuned to the Holy Spirit who guides the Church into the fullness of truth (cf. Jn 16:13; *Lumen Gentium,* 4), and produces in her the fruits of his action, which Saint Paul lists as "love, joy, peace, patient endurance, kindness, generosity, faith, mildness and chastity" (Gal 5:22-23). And since the Holy Spirit has placed in the Church the special pastoral charism of the Magisterium, we know that *adherence to the Magisterium is an indispensable condition for a correct reading of "the signs of the times"* and hence a condition for the supernatural fruitfulness of all ministries in the Church.

171. You indeed have an important role in the Church's dialogue with the complex and varied cultural environment of the United States. The first law of this dialogue is *fidelity to Christ and to his Church.* And in this fundamental act of faith and trust you already show the world the basis of your special position within the community of God's people. Also required for this dialogue is *a true understanding of the values involved in America's historical experience.* At the same time the Christian concepts of the common good, of virtue and conscience, of liberty and justice, must be distinguished from what is sometimes inadequately presented as the expression of these realities. As religious, you are especially sensitive to the implications of this dialogue with the world in which you are called to live and work. As men and women consecrated to God, you are aware of having a special responsibility to be a sign—an authentic prophetic sign—that will speak to the Church and to the world, not in terms of easy condemnation, but humbly *showing forth the power of God's Word to heal and uplift, to unite and bind with love.*

172. At this important moment of the history of the human family it is essential for the Church to proclaim the full truth about God—Father, Son and Holy Spirit—and the full truth about our human condition and destiny as revealed in Christ and authentically transmitted through the teaching of the Church. The faithful have the right to receive the true teaching of the Church in its

purity and integrity, with all its demands and power. When people are looking for a sure point of reference for their own values and their ethical choices, they turn to the special witnesses of the Church's holiness and justice—to you religious. They expect and want to be convinced by the example of your acceptance of God's Word.

173. Dear sisters and brothers: *the life we now live is not our own; Christ is living in us.* We still live our human life, but it is a life of faith in the Son of God, who loved us and gave himself for us (cf. Gal 2:20). In these words Saint Paul sums up the core of our Christian experience, and even more so *the heart of religious life.* The validity and fruitfulness of religious life depends upon *union with Jesus Christ.*

Union with Christ demands *a true interior life of prayer,* a life of closeness to him. At the same time it enables you to be effective witnesses before the world of the healing and liberating power of the Paschal Mystery. It means that above all in your own lives and in your own communities the Paschal Mystery is first being celebrated and experienced through *the Eucharist and the sacrament of Penance.* In this way your works of charity and justice, of mercy and compassion will be true signs of Christ's presence in the world.

174. The challenges which you faced yesterday you will face again tomorrow. The thousand tasks that now draw upon your courage and your energies will hardly disappear next week, next month, next year. What then is the meaning of our meeting? What "word of the Lord" is addressed to us here? As the one who for the time being has been given the place of the Fisherman from Galilee, as the one who occupies the Chair of Peter for this fleeting hour in the Church's life, allow me to make my own the sentiments of the reading from our Evening Prayer: *"Be examples to the flock"* (1 Pt 5:3)—examples of faith and charity, of hope and joy, of obedience, sacrifice and humble service. And "when the Chief Shepherd appears, you will win for yourselves the unfading crown of glory" (v. 4).

175. To the *contemplative religious* of the United States, whose lives are hidden with Christ in God, I wish to say a word of profound thanks for reminding us that "here we have no lasting city" (Heb 13:14), and that all life must be lived in the heart of the living God. May the whole Church in this land recognize the primacy and efficacy of the spiritual values which you represent. The Second Vatican Council deliberately chose to call you "the glory of the Church" (*Perfectae Caritatis,* 7). Brothers and sisters, men and women religious of the United States: your country needs the witness of your deep spirituality and your commitment to the life-giving power of the Gospel. America needs to see all the power of love in your hearts expressed in evangelizing zeal. The whole world needs to discover in you "the kindness and love of God our Savior" (Tit 3:4). Go forward, therefore, in the mystery of the dying and rising of Jesus. *Go forward in faith, hope and charity, spending yourselves in the Church's mission of evangelization and service.* Always be examples to the flock. And know that "when the Chief Shepherd appears, you will win for yourselves the unfading crown of glory" (1 Pt 5:4).

176. In this Marian Year of grace may you find joy and strength in an ever greater devotion to Mary, the Virgin Mother of the Redeemer. As "the model and protectress of all consecrated life" (can. 663, par. 4) may she lead each one of you to perfect union with her Son, our Lord Jesus Christ, and to ever closer collaboration in his redemptive mission. And may the example of *Mary's discipleship* confirm you all in generosity and love.

12

TO THE GENERAL CHAPTERS OF THE CISTERCIAN MONKS AND NUNS OF THE STRICT OBSERVANCE

December 17, 1987

177. Responding to the desire you expressed to demonstrate your filial affection and faithful devotion towards the Successor of Peter, I gladly receive you today, dear brothers and sisters of the Order of the Cistercians of the Strict Observance, on the exceptional occasion offered by the simultaneous celebration of your respective General Chapters.

I am particularly happy to greet among you the abbots and abbesses and the delegated representatives of the approximately 150 monasteries with more than five thousand monks and nuns spread throughout the world. All the members of your great family have their eyes and hearts fixed on you at the present time. They await from you the decisions which will help them to live out, in ever greater authenticity, the magnificent vocation to which they have been called.

178. Indeed, the Second Vatican Council, in the decree *Perfectae Caritatis,* insists on the eminent place of the wholly contemplative life in the Mystical Body of Christ. The members of these communities "offer to God a lofty sacrifice of praise; they illumine the People of God by abundant fruits of holiness, they win it over by their example and obtain its growth by a hidden apostolic fruitfulness. They are thus the honor of the Church and a source of heavenly graces" (n. 7).

179. Monks and nuns, you center your contemplative life on constant prayer, the expression of your love for God and humanity. In silence and solitude, you live this

prayer in monasteries which you rarely leave, protected by the discipline of the cloister which is freely and resolutely desired for the great spiritual good it brings. You joyfully accept great austerity because it powerfully aids you to center yourselves on that which is essential and it unites you more intimately to Christ.

180. All of you, Cistercians of the Strict Observance, following in the footsteps of Saint Bernard, strive to put into practice the Benedictine Rule in its integrity. You seek God in the imitation of Christ under the leadership of your superiors according to the *Charter of Charity,* which establishes the forms of your vocation properly authenticated by the Church.

Sons and daughters of Saint Benedict, you are convinced that nothing must be preferred to the "work of God." By the celebration of the Divine Office, you offer him the sacrifice of praise and you intercede for the salvation of the world.

181. On the other hand, *lectio divina,* through the meditation on the Word of God, is for you the wellspring of prayer and the school of contemplation. The *Charter of Charity* emphasizes as well the fraternal charity which unites you. You are concerned that "no one be troubled or saddened in the house of God" (Saint Benedict), and that every cloister be a place where one experiences that "it is good for brothers to dwell in unity" (cf. Ps 133:1).

182. Monks and nuns, you belong to the same spiritual family and you share the same monastic heritage which you must preserve. You cooperate and you assist one another while taking into account your respective autonomy and the arrangements provided by the Church.

It is in this spirit that the Holy See, faithful to the conciliar teachings on the woman's place in today's world, has, since 1970, allowed the female branch of your Order to have its own General Chapter in order to deal with the particular questions which concern it and especially to study and draw up its own legislation.

183. For the past several years, in order to respond to the provisions of the "motu proprio" *Ecclesiae Sanctae,* you have worked on both sides for the elaboration of your drafts of constitutions to be submitted for the approval of the Holy See.

As this task was reaching its completion, you took the initiative of convoking your two General Chapters in Rome in separate sessions but with the possibility for contacts, in order to render easier the final elaboration of the fundamental elements common to the two branches. I hope together with you that the drafts thus established, responding to the required conditions, will be able to serve as norms of life for the monks as well as for the nuns.

184. You are bringing your labors to a close during Advent, at the moment when the Church is preparing herself in a more immediate way to receive the Savior. This time is entirely filled with the presence of Mary, the Mother of God and resplendent Icon of the Church, towards whom Saint Bernard showed the ardent and filial devotion which has remained fully in the heritage of your Order.

I ask you to carry into your monasteries, to all your brothers and sisters, and in particular to the sick and infirm, my greetings, my affectionate encouragement and my blessing. I pray the Virgin Mary to guide you and to assist you all in your life consecrated to Christ and to the Church.

And I bless you in the Lord's name.

13

TO THE BROTHERS OF CHRISTIAN INSTRUCTION OF PLOERMEL

March 25, 1988

185. In receiving you here, I have the happy impression of contemplating more than one hundred and sixty years of teaching and evangelization of children and adolescents. Once again, the Church warmly thanks the Brothers of Ploërmel. In the mystery of life after death, your beloved founders, Fathers Jean-Marie de La Mennais and Gabriel Deshayes, are rejoicing at the vitality of their Institute. Indeed, I know of your concern regarding vocations. I am equally aware that Africa gives you hope. The branches of the Institute founded not long ago in Uganda, Rwanda, and Zaire have already borne some good fruit. Although I am happy to receive you all, allow me to greet especially our dear Brother Bernard Gaudel, whom you have just reelected as Superior General, as a mark of your confidence in him. I assure him of my fervent and prayerful best wishes for a most fruitful accomplishment of his ministry of service and authority. Dear Brother Bernard, since I know your home, Cancale, in the Bay of Mont-Saint-Michel, I know that you can count on the intercession of your admirable compatriot, Blessed Jeanne Jugan, to watch over you.

186. During this *General Chapter* which is coming to an end, you have studied intensely your Rule of life, which was earlier brought up to date and approved by the Congregation for Religious in 1983. It is true that, even if the texts express well *your special charism,* there is always room to deepen their spiritual sense in order to renew your manner of daily life. This particular gift, received from your founders, is the ardent search for, and intimate encounter with the Lord Jesus, who is contem-

plated, invoked and loved without measure. It is thus, and only thus, that the Brothers will discover the way which Christ is showing them and along which he calls all your communities and the Institute itself to follow.

187. This means of personal and communal sanctification, realized better and better, allows you to give a *shining and stimulating witness* to those who see you live as men of prayer and of interior life. With enthusiasm and humility, share your love of Jesus Christ, your riches of faith, hope and charity, the theological virtues concretely lived, with all the youths entrusted to your care, with their parents, with the Christian laity who have accepted in conscience to collaborate in the educational aim of your schools and colleges. You thus contribute to the vitality and the sanctification of the People of God according to the original form inspired in your founders by the Spirit of the Lord. The Lord has mysteriously chosen you for the most beautiful work there is: preparing youth in the best possible way for the future and the many services to society in accordance with the Gospel message, which is always relevant, inexhaustible and life-giving.

188. As witnesses to the Kingdom of God by your religious consecration, you live this radical gift through your responsibilities as teachers and educators. Your Institute has been raised up in the Church for this mission of primary importance: to make Christ and his Good News known through schools. Our age, marked by important socio-cultural upheavals, urgently demands an evangelization of intellects at all levels of knowledge. Therefore, free from the slightest doubt, you must remain completely faithful to your charism as well as to this prudent yet bold sense of adaptation to conditions of life and to cultures in which your apostolate is exercised. The Church expects you to be firmly attached to your educational mission both in the countries of ancient Christian civilization as well as in regions where Christianity has a much more recent history.

189. For more than one hundred and fifty years, the Brothers of Ploërmel have faced with exemplary courage the difficulties of the missionary apostolate under very challenging conditions. *Today,* the Church calls upon you to take up the same challenges *in different contexts.* I am thinking of the pervading practical and reductionist materialism; I think also of oppressive socio-political situations. Dear Brothers, with the Lord's powerful aid and thanks to a high level of theological, spiritual, intellectual and technological formation, you will be able to respond to the profound and considerable needs of young people, to that which they expect from you, sometimes unconsciously, in catechesis and spiritual life as well as in the domain of human culture in all its forms.

190. Finally, your noble mission of education and sanctification is to be carried out in a vigorous spirit of perfect communion among yourselves and with the entire People of God. I am aware of your Institute's unfailing fidelity to the See of Peter and to the Magisterium of the Popes. It is a precious heritage of your founders. I heartily and confidently encourage you to continue to develop your effective collaboration with the episcopal conferences and the pastors of the diocese or the parishes who have summoned you, with the Christian laity, young and adult. This "sensus Ecclesiae" will ever be your great strength and the unmistakable sign of your ecclesial commitment on behalf of the people of our time.

At the conclusion of this meeting I invoke God's choicest blessings on the entire Congregation, on its leaders, on the elderly or infirm Brothers, on those responsible for the formation of candidates, on all the laity who collaborate in your magnificent work and on all the youths and their families. I entrust them all to the maternal protection of the Mother of Christ, the Redeemer.

14

TO THE ITALIAN UNION OF MAJOR SUPERIORS, IN ROME

April 9, 1988

191. You have begun your meeting by praying together to Our Lady in the Basilica of Saint Mary Major, before the precious icon of Mary, Mother of the Church, venerated in the headquarters of the Italian Union of Major Superiors (USMI). After reflecting on the theme: "Consecrated women in the Church for the salvation of the world," and taking part in various doctrinal conferences, informative sessions, and elections, you conclude your important assembly today with this audience.

I am very pleased to receive you. I greet you all most cordially and thank you for your presence, which I know is animated by deep faith and a lively ecclesial sense. I extend my affectionate and appreciative regards through you to all your sisters.

Looking at you and seeing in you all your religious communities, one spontaneously thinks of the great good which the various Congregations have achieved and continue to achieve to the advantage of souls and of society.

192. In fact, every Congregation has a long history of activity and achievements, which, beginning with the founders and foundresses, extends through the span of decades and also centuries, witnessing to God's love and presence amid the tribulations of the human pilgrimage on earth. It is not difficult, but moving, to imagine the wonderful array of religious, who, in the past and still today, serve in constant and total dedication, with love and attention to persons, in schools, hospices, hospitals, prisons; in peace and in war; among the poor, the disabled, the elderly; at the service of parishes, priests, seminaries. Strong, kind, brave, always self-sacrificing because they

are consecrated, sometimes tired, yet generous—how much the sisters have accomplished in Christ's name and for love of him!

193. If in this perspective there is reason for sadness, it is that, unfortunately, many works are abandoned today; many houses are closed through a lack of young members, of new vocations. However, one must not lose heart but continue to trust in the Lord. One must pray insistently to him that his call to total self-giving, which certainly continues to make itself heard, may be accepted by a growing number of young people, and that, at the same time, priests may be wise and enlightened in their work of formation and spiritual direction.

194. In the light of so much past experience, one might aptly say that the sisters in every Congregation are truly "women consecrated in the Church for the salvation of the world." They always combine the witness of their own Christian faith with the practice of charity, according to the orientation of their particular charism. I sincerely hope that, through the USMI, unity of purpose and mutual understanding between the various communities may continue and grow, so that they may complement one another and work together in mutual charity and edification.

195. What is to be done today, amid the difficulties of the modern world, to revive the commitment of consecrated persons and to increase vocations in all the Congregations? The question can sometimes become worrisome and painful; yet in the decree *Perfectae Caritatis* the Second Vatican Council has already indicated the only possible and effective response: "Amid such a great variety of gifts, however, all those who are called by God to the practice of the evangelical counsels, and who make faithful profession of them, bind themselves to the Lord in a special way. They follow Christ who, virginal and poor, redeemed and sanctified mankind by obedience unto death

on the cross. Under the impulse of love, which the Holy Spirit pours into their hearts, they live more and more for Christ and for his Body, the Church. The more fervently, therefore, they join themselves to Christ by this gift of their whole life, the fuller does the Church's life become and the more vigorous and fruitful her apostolate" (n. 1).

196. One must be inspired constantly by these simple and clear words, in order to draw light and comfort from them. They tell us that in the person of the religious there is a "sacramental consecration" which comes through baptism and confirmation, and a "religious consecration" which comes through profession of the vows, following the call of vocation. Both "consecrations" are divine works, but they also require human collaboration. "Religious consecration" has its deep roots in the "sacramental consecration," but it has its own new and completely special title, because it is expressed in total self-giving to God after the example of Christ, poor, chaste, obedient: it is realized in the service of the Church by proclaiming the Gospel, saving souls, and by totally and constantly living the truth. In all this the religious sister finds in Mary the highest model, and above all, help and strength in moments of difficulty and danger.

197. Amid the din of so many discordant voices, one perceives today with greater urgency the need for clarity in support of a choice such as yours, which supposes the gift of one's life without reserve to the Christian ideal. The Second Vatican Council vigorously states that what was valid for consecrated life in the past still remains true and will always be so, because it rests on a foundation which does not change: the salvation of the world according to the providential design of creation and redemption which Jesus revealed and the Church perennially teaches.

198. In this connection, I would like to recall a reflection of Blessed Teresa Benedicta of the Cross, the Carmelite martyr at Auschwitz: "To give oneself to God,

completely forgetful of self, not to take account of one's own individual life in order to leave room for God's life: here is the fundamental motive, the beginning and end of religious life. The more fully this is realized, the richer the divine life which fills the soul. However, this divine life is love, an overflowing love which has no limits and gives itself willingly; a love which is responsive to every need; a love which restores the sick to health and awakens the spiritually dead; a love which protects, defends, nourishes, teaches and forms; a love which suffers with the afflicted and rejoices with the joyful, which is ready to serve everybody in order to fulfill the Father's design: in a word, the love of the Divine Heart."

199. The sisters in the various Congregations must realize this today also, with a vivid sense of the communal character of the apostolate, on the local and universal levels. Therefore, in your houses, be bearers of hope and trust! Have confidence in the Church, because this means having confidence in Christ, dead and risen, who has promised temporal indefectibility and doctrinal infallibility to the Church. It means having confidence in the Holy Spirit, present to enlighten minds and sanctify souls through "grace" which operates in the secrecy of consciences. The work of grace is certain, real, sure, even if it also demands that the seed fallen on the ground die in order to bear fruit. The pasch of the resurrection must be preceded by the agony of Gethsemane and the pangs of the crucifixion. Know how to look with optimism and hope on the consoling realities which still exist in the Church and in society today: they are great and abundant, and show that love, and therefore God, conquers in the end.

200. May Our Lady, who always accompanies you and whom you invoke with love and trust, maintain in you a strong and ardent commitment to self-giving, so that the ideals of a life of faith, charity, goodness and holiness—the only ideals which provide support—may triumph.

May my apostolic blessing encourage you; I now impart it to you with all my heart, and willingly extend it to all your sisters.

15

TO PRIESTS AND RELIGIOUS IN VERONA (ITALY)

April 16, 1988

201. I greet you most cordially! Following my official greeting to the citizens, I am delighted to begin with you my pastoral visit to this ancient and glorious portion of Christ's flock which is the Church of Verona. I find the choice of this cathedral as our meeting place significant and appropriate, since you are celebrating the eighth centenary of the dedication of this temple by Pope Urban III on September 13, 1187. However, if we consider the constructions on this site which preceded the present cathedral, we can go back to the time of the glorious Saint Zeno, the eighth bishop and patron of this diocese. In the fourth century, precisely on this spot, he ordered the construction of the first mother church of the Christian community which he had baptized and led to the truth of Christ: *"Veronam praedicando reduxit ad baptismum" (Rhythmus Papinianus).* (...)

202. Dear brothers and sisters, how eloquent is this meeting of ours today in the principal temple of the diocese! In the midst of the People of God, you are, and must be, in a special way, *"men and women of the temple."* Your vocation, in fact, links you closely to the "house of the Lord" and to "the place where his glory dwells" (Ps 26 [25]: 8).

You are called in a special way to help people understand the beauty and importance of divine worship and of the holy place where the mysteries of salvation are celebrated. How well this cathedral, with its extraordinary beauty, facilitates this task, this mission of yours! How well it represents and expresses it! In these stones, in these precious works of art laden with the centuries, one might almost say that faith itself becomes visible. In and through them is expressed—with an extraordinary evocative power and through the charm of art and poetry—the genius and inventiveness of man, who in his works desires to praise God; in so doing, he offers the fullest measure of himself and of his spirit made in the image of God!

203. Your vocation to lead people to God is certainly splendid; it carries with it, as you well know, a *responsibility.* The words of the psalmist are, in fact, well known: "Who shall ascend the mountain of the Lord? And who shall stand in his holy place? He who has clean hands and a pure heart, who does not lift up his soul to what is false, and does not swear deceitfully. He will receive a blessing from the Lord, a reward from God his savior" (Ps 24 [23]:3-5).

204. The purer and more irreproachable your lives, the more your conduct corresponds with the mysteries you celebrate and the prayers you offer to the Most High, the more successfully will you help so many of our contemporaries, distracted by secularist indifference, to understand the importance and indeed the necessity of a divine worship which is both interior and exterior. You must help today's men and women to regain appreciation, love, and respect for holy places, where the Christian community celebrates and adores the *Eucharistic mystery* under the presiding priest.

205. The cathedral takes on particular importance from this point of view, due to the fact that the gathering of the holy people of God takes place with the *bishop* presiding, the *pastor of the diocese,* the one who, in communion with the universal Church and under the guidance of the Successor of Peter, is in his Church the supreme guardian and minister of the divine mysteries, the one who is the foundation and the guarantee of ecclesial unity in the plurality of ministries and charisms. Hence the cathedral is the *chosen place* for the gathering of the local Church, into which you, brothers and sisters,

are called to bring your witness by manifesting in your lives an *especially close rapport with the bishop* and, at the same time, with those, both inside and outside the ecclesial community, who have *particular need of the divine mercy and of fraternal solidarity.*

206. That is why our meeting today in this temple is so profoundly significant, both for you and for me. What better place, in fact, than the cathedral church to express the unity of the local Church in communion with the Successor of Peter? Where could you, in particular, "men and women of the temple," have been better able to express this communion than in your own cathedral church?

In it, as in every Catholic church, God makes himself present and active—in accordance with his express will—in a special way, above all *when the sacraments are celebrated,* particularly the *sacrament of the Eucharist.* Through this sacrament one can truly say that God *dwells,* even if in a very mysterious way, in his temple. In his temple, in the tabernacle, we can always meet and contemplate him beyond the veil of the Eucharistic species. Thus we can find consolation in the midst of suffering, enlightenment in our doubts and uncertainties, and inspiration for new initiatives of charity.

207. Any apostolic activity which does not flow from this love for the temple and for the sacramental Jesus rapidly degenerates into an empty activism and remains tarnished by earthly ambitions. It thus deprives itself of that supernatural foundation which alone permits it to have a true and lasting impact on souls.

However, God's temple, as Saint Zeno said, is also the *People of God,* the souls who are in God's grace. *Jesus dwells in the tabernacle that he may dwell in people's hearts.* He loves the temple made of stone, but he loves above all the temple made of flesh which we constitute—as long, that is, as we wish to receive him with purity of heart. It was this consideration which moved Saint Zeno to tell his faithful with emotion: "Incomparably glorious and truly worthy of God is the fact that, with one sentiment and one faith, the one praying for the other, the priest and the temple (that is, the believing people) turn to God with the same devotion." And, speaking of the temple of stone in which we find ourselves, he exhorted the faithful who were present: "Rejoice, then, O faithful people, and learn to build the edifice of your persons from this new temple which you have crowded with your consoling presence in such great numbers. From the very fact that this edifice cannot contain you, we can see that your faith contains God" (*Discourse* II, 6, 2-5).

208. Faith cannot but express itself in the gathering of the community in the Lord's temple. Divine worship and works of fraternal charity are the indissoluble signs of true faith, of a faith that does not separate adoration of the Creator from dedication to creatures, or the absolute gift of self to the Creator from the judicious appreciation of finite realities, without either confusing or separating them. The mystery of the Incarnation teaches us how to unite them while maintaining their distinction.

209. Dear brothers and sisters, may you see yourselves as *promoters of the true faith,* with humility and courage, in communion with the bishop and with the Church, in a true spirit of service to souls. Today there is such need of this, at all levels of society. *Catechesis for adults and catechesis for the young. Catechesis for everyone.* In this regard, I make my own the words that Saint Zeno addressed to his faithful as he exhorted them to cultivate and deepen the theological virtue of faith: "We must embrace it with tenacity and safeguard it with every sort of virtue. We must apply ourselves to it with courage. In fact, it is the solid foundation of our life, our invincible bulwark and, at the same time, our weapon against the attacks of the devil, the impenetrable armor of our soul, the true and concise science of the law, the terror of demons, the courage of the martyrs, the beauty and the rampart of the

Church, the ministry of God, the friend of Christ, the table companion of the Holy Spirit" (*Discourse* I, 36, 3-7).

210. Let us ask ourselves whether we do not at times relativize the truths of faith even as we absolutize the ideologies of this world. It is with the Gospel that we must judge the world, never accommodating the message of Christ to the opinions of the day.

You are all aware of how urgent a need there is for a *re-evangelization of the peoples of ancient Christian faith.* This is one of the primary tasks of the Church today. You, precisely as priests and religious, clearly must feel personally committed and present in the front lines.

211. In serving the firm establishment and the spread of the faith, each of you has a specific task to perform: *the priest,* through the administration of the sacraments, the mandate of official preaching and the role of presiding over the believing community; *the consecrated religious,* first of all through the example of a penitent, mortified, irreproachable life profoundly dedicated to God according to the charism of his or her Institute: if of active life, then in the works of the external apostolate; if of contemplative life, through the sacrifice of self in silence, solitude and prayer.

212. May each of you fulfill properly the particular vocation to which you have been called, feeling yourself a living member of the Mystical Body. In this way, your activity will attain its due efficacy in harmony with the activity of others.

The Marian Year which we are celebrating presents Our Lady to us as the one who interiorizes her faith to the fullest, she who fully becomes "an interior space for the Word and the blessing of the Father" (*Redemptoris Mater,* 28), as the one who makes the pilgrimage of faith not without the particular "labor of the heart" which that pilgrimage demands (cf. *ibid.,* 17).

213. May you *women religious,* in particular, feel challenged by the example of Mary. She is clearly the model for every Christian; but how can we fail to recognize in consecrated womanhood, in a woman who is a Christian virgin, a wholly special sign of Mary's presence in the world? You women religious are called in a special way to make Mary's maternal love tangible to mankind. This is your special and irreplaceable role in the Church. It is here that you give the best of yourselves in carrying out your own mission, as women, in the plan of salvation.

214. May the Blessed Virgin, whom you venerate here under the title of "Madonna of the people," suggest to you and to all of us the attitudes which are most fitting for our encounter with the Lord in the temple of our heart and for the effectiveness of our witness of faith in the temple of our Christian communities.

With these wishes and sentiments, I assure you of all my affection and I give you a heartfelt and special blessing, which I extend to all your loved ones as well as to your fellow priests and religious who were unable to participate in the joy of this meeting.

16

TO WOMEN RELIGIOUS IN LA PAZ (BOLIVIA)

May 10, 1988

215. I greet you with much affection and I thank you for being here. Many of you have come from very distant places, certainly not without sacrifice on your part, as well as on the part of the sisters who had to stay behind and take your places during your absence. To all of you I want to express my most intense gratitude for the selfless work which you are doing, sometimes amid great difficulties, especially in favor of the poorest and the marginalized; in catechesis, direct pastoral action, health assistance, human development, education, vocations; singling out your active presence in hospitals, orphanages, and homes for the elderly, and in the centers of prayer and liturgical celebration.

216. Having heard the reading of the Gospel, in which Mary, full of grace, sings God's praises, I invite you to *meditate on the Word of God with me* with the same attitude of the Blessed Virgin, that is, ready to listen with faithfulness and to respond with generosity.

In order that we may be light to enlighten those around us with the force of the Gospel, we need to meditate frequently on the Word of God in periods of intense prayer, through which consecrated persons continue to make themselves more and more capable of giving and surrendering. Certainly, that capacity for self-giving is born of the divine Word and of the strength of the Holy Spirit.

217. The humble attitude of listening, prayer and surrender of the Virgin of the "Magnificat," will always be the pattern and model for every consecrated life. Mary's union with Christ the Redeemer, ceaselessly supported by

her faithfulness to the divine Word, is the secret of her existence as an image of the Church: "To believe means 'to abandon oneself' to the truth of the Word of the living God, knowing and humbly acknowledging 'how unsearchable are his judgments and how inscrutable his ways' (Rom 11:33). Mary, who by the eternal will of the Most High stands, one may say, at the very center of those 'inscrutable ways' and 'unsearchable judgments' of God, conforms herself to them in the dim light of faith, accepting fully and with a ready heart everything that is decreed in the divine plan" (*Redemptoris Mater,* 14). Are these not the same plans that God himself has made for you, beloved sisters?

218. If you really want to be of help to your brothers and sisters, and to the needy first of all, you will have to shape your lives daily as a personal offering to Christ, who continues to offer himself in the Eucharist, associating yourselves, at the same time, with his work of redemption. In meditation of the Word and in the Eucharistic celebration it is always Jesus, the "Bread of Life," who comes to us to make us like him (Jn 6:35, 48). Your "yes" to the Word of God and your association with Christ in the economy of redemption follow the footsteps of Mary who "devoted herself totally as a handmaid of the Lord to the person and work of her Son" (*Lumen Gentium,* 56).

219. I want to congratulate you for your *fidelity to, and communion with, the Church,* with the Pope and the bishops, each of whom is, according to the expression of the Second Vatican Council, the "principle and foundation of unity in his particular Church, fashioned after the model of the universal Church" (*Lumen Gentium,* 23). Your responsible collaboration with them and with the priests and laity in the tasks of evangelization increase in the religious life the sense of participation in the sacramental nature of the Church as mystery, communion and mission.

220. The consecrated person worthily represents the Church as the virgin who awaits, with her lamp burning, the bridegroom's arrival. To maintain throughout a lifetime this attitude of one who guards a great treasure is a special testimony for the Church and "a privileged means of effective evangelization" (*Evangelii Nuntiandi,* 69). Actually, religious profession has consecrated you to the service of others, in their concrete situation and in the perspective of eschatological hope, that is, looking towards the final coming of the Lord (Mt 25:6; Rev 3:20). Your ability to insert yourselves into the most varied human situations will also depend on your manner of living this Christian hope.

221. This attitude of unconditional and responsible service to the Church will help you discover and proclaim the special place and dignity of women in today's world. "In the light of Mary, the Church sees in the face of women the reflection of a beauty which mirrors the loftiest sentiments of which the human heart is capable: the fullness of self-giving inspired by love; the strength that is capable of bearing the greatest sorrows; limitless fidelity and tireless devotion to work; the ability to combine penetrating intuition with words of support and encouragement" (*Redemptoris Mater,* 46).

222. Having been consecrated to God, therefore, through Christ the Bridegroom in the charity of the Holy Spirit, you should make your lives shine like a light, or a transparency, by your way of loving and serving Jesus. Yes, it is in the *following of Jesus* that we find the essence and the summit of religious life, as it were: "...go, sell everything you have and give it to the poor; then, come and follow me" (Mk 10:21). Your prophetic presence as consecrated persons in the world, in harmony with the charism of your own Institute, will be a continuing and hope-giving sign of this evangelical following of Jesus, with the special characteristic of being light and salt, sign and encouragement that are distinctive of the spirit of the Sermon on the Mount.

223. Another witness that you must give to the People of God is *community life,* as an effective sign of evangelization (cf. Jn 17:23). This is an indispensable element of religious life, a characteristic which all religious Institutes have had from the beginning. Spiritual bonds cannot develop and remain except through daily and continuous relationships in the life of fraternity. On the other hand, community life is also an effective aid for perseverance in the evangelical following of Jesus.

The activities proper to common life, animated by Gospel charity, have as their point of convergence the personal relationship with Christ and consequently, with the mystery of the Church, which is the mystery of communion and sharing. Therefore, put every effort into cultivating community life, in order to strengthen it and make it more pleasing, so that it will become a precious means of mutual help and an unsurpassable way of achieving personal fulfillment. This entails that all members are fortified in the same resolve to become witnesses to evangelical charity, as was experienced in the primitive ecclesial communities: "The whole group of believers was united, heart and soul; no one claimed for his own use anything that he had, as everything they owned was held in common" (Acts 4:32). In fact (their) unity "shows that Christ has come (cf. Jn 13:35; 17:21); from it results great apostolic influence" (*Perfectae Caritatis,* 15).

224. As in other places in Latin America, here too *the poor* suffer all kinds of privations. Much too often they lack what is indispensable for living as human beings and children of God. There are farmers, miners and many other workers and residents of the *barrios* around the cities who do not even earn enough to feed their children. There are also the new poor and the newly marginalized persons, victims of a materialistic society which puts in the heart of the families, the workers and youth, the unbridled search for comfort, profit and power as the main goal, and is the cause of all violence and oppression (cf. *Sollicitudo Rei Socialis,* 37).

225. Each one of you, according to your own particular charism, should be at the service of the poor, in whom Jesus is present in a special and preferential way. Christ awaits you in the different fields where charity must be exercised with total generosity. Your faithfulness to the divine Word, your daily living of the redemptive mystery present in the Eucharist and your evangelical following of Christ, will make you discover new fields of evangelization and at the same time make you ready to offer your whole life to these services of charity and mission.

226. One of the consequences of poverty in Bolivia is the lack of education in general, but particularly in rural areas and in the *barrios* and sectors around the cities, where living conditions are more precarious. I know that many of you are working directly at the service of the poorest of the people through the "Fe y Alegria" movement, while others are involved in other services of the pastoral ministry and education. A special area for your work in favor of these needy areas is your collaboration with those who are responsible, such as educators, community leaders, catechists, etc. It is necessary at all times to encourage these men and women working with you so that they will continue to work without discouragement and with the spirit and generosity of the Gospel. Every evangelizer, whether lay, priest, or consecrated person, should approach the poor with a "meek and humble" heart which seeks the light of the Gospel, and with a poor life which does not seek self-interest or impose personal criteria.

227. You must not forget that the *witness of your lives* is very important in a society tempted to switch values and seek first security and personal well-being, to have and possess more. As women religious, you are to give witness to the Gospel values which redeem the total person. The witness of your lives in following the chaste, poor and obedient Christ reveals the false security of the

goods of this world, when they are preferred to the true good of the person and the community.

In the light of Christ, who is the Way, the Truth and the Life, it is clear that a human being "cannot fully find himself except through a sincere gift of himself" (*Gaudium et Spes,* 24). In the context of the Gospel teaching to which you witness, one can understand why "a person is more precious for what he is than for what he has" (*Gaudium et Spes,* 35).

228. For this reason, true wealth does not consist in having things nor even in giving them, but in the capacity to give of oneself and, consequently, to be able to share oneself with those who suffer and seek the truth. Your virginity, poverty and obedience are a sign of the way to love Jesus: to seek to share the lot of one's brothers and sisters in solidarity, to give oneself, no longer to belong to oneself, to follow always the salvific plan of the Father. By your life you are "like a sign of charity and a stimulus towards it as well as a unique fountain of spiritual fertility in the world" (*Lumen Gentium,* 42).

229. Your life will have an evangelizing value if the transparent life witness of your consecration and your capacity for a personal relationship with Christ in following him are translated into action in the mission field. May the poor feel the solidarity of the one who gives of herself; may the lonely and abandoned experience a new presence; may the voiceless discover that there is someone who listens to them with kindness; in a word, may all find in you a personal sign of the presence and love of Christ who "went about doing good" (Acts 10:38).

230. *The living out of the evangelical counsels* has a direct connection with the Kingdom and is an eschatological sign of its beginning already in and through the Church, knowing that its fullness will be achieved only in the other life. You are the qualified witnesses of the Kingdom, both in its present existence as well as its future form. "The

Church, consequently, equipped with the gifts of her Founder and faithfully guarding his precepts of charity, humility and self-sacrifice, receives the mission to proclaim and establish among all peoples the Kingdom of Christ and of God. She becomes on earth the initial budding forth of that Kingdom. While she slowly grows, the Church strains towards the consummation of the Kingdom and, with all her strength, hopes and desires to be united in glory with her King" (*Lumen Gentium,* 5).

231. Evangelization cannot prescind from, but should take into consideration the real situation, which must be illuminated by the Gospel message, to arouse in the heart of every person the hunger and thirst for true justice and the hope of the liberation of the entire person.

Every religious institution should be open to work together with others, to share the goods it receives, fortify the services it offers and work in harmony in the joint pastoral action and life of the local Church. The formation and strengthening of one's own charism, which are received principally in one's own Institute, should not impede prudent participation in intercongregational formation, when this has been established by the religious and ecclesiastical superiors.

232. Your lives and works are a very important part of the ecclesial reality. The Church needs you for the service of her evangelizing activity, as persons who responsibly share in her mystery and mission. So that your works and initiatives may continue, it is necessary that many young women also hear the Lord's call and decide to follow it by means of a total consecration to him. The testimony of your consecrated life and the example of service to others, carried out in the joy of the disciple who loves the Lord, will be very important in the *promotion of vocations.*

233. In Bolivia, approximately 60 percent of women religious are from other countries, while only 40 percent are Bolivians. Naturally, every vocation is always part of the

one ecclesial family in which there are no foreigners; however, it is very important that the work for the promotion of *native vocations* be intensified, so that evangelization can more effectively reach the heart of each of the varied and rich cultures in this beloved land. A vocation is a gift from God, and the entire ecclesial community should become a community praying for vocations. The work related to the promotion of vocations must be harmonious and inclusive, aimed at helping young women to open their hearts generously to the Lord's call.

234. I invite you, then, to the practice of *fervent and persevering prayer,* as an expression of your love and following of Christ.

Following Christ is something existential; the promises made to practice the evangelical counsels are the clearest way to express this following and imitation of Christ, union and relationship with him, configuration and transformation into him. One follows Christ and extends his presence in time, being just as he was: chaste, obedient, poor, humble, sacrificed, totally given to the Father's plan for the salvation of mankind. This reality of consecrated life as a kind of prolongation of Christ in history is beyond human understanding and surpasses human strength; it can only be possible through *intense periods of prayer* and silent and fervent contemplation. Women religious of the active life should be contemplatives from these intense periods of prayer so that they can also be contemplatives in action.

235. From the earliest times, consecrated life in the form of the *cloistered contemplative life* has existed in the Church. Cloistered nuns were the first women religious to come to Bolivia, and I address to them now my affectionate greeting and my exhortation to the radical following of, and espousal to Christ, to prayer and to profound harmony with the Church's mission. They "will always have a distinguished part to play in Christ's Mystical Body...and by imparting a hidden apostolic fruitfulness, they make

(it) grow" *(Perfectae Caritatis,* 7). Their lifestyle has been, is and will always be valued by the Church because it is a stimulus for the contemplative and eschatological dimension of the entire People of God. My dear contemplative sisters, you have entered into a "dynamism, whose impulse is love" (*Evangelica Testificatio,* 8), which makes you take upon yourselves in a more radical way the needs of all mankind. You are "the love in the heart of the Church," as Saint Therese of Lisieux, patroness of the missions, wanted to be, because, living in the heart of God, you live more closely than anyone else to "the joys and hopes, the griefs and anguish of the people of our time" (*Gaudium et Spes,* 1). The abundance and quality of the other vocations to the consecrated life and priesthood depend to a great extent on your generous and joyful fidelity to the contemplative and cloistered life.

236. The *Marian Year,* my dear sisters, should be the starting point of an enthusiastic journey towards the third millennium, when the Church feels the need and the powerful urgency to be a clear sign of the Beatitudes. I express to you my wish that, with your eyes fixed on Mary—the consecrated woman *par excellence,* as figure of your espousal to Christ—you may come to possess during these years an ever deeper knowledge of the conciliar and postconciliar teaching on the consecrated life; may it be transformed for you into a true "Marian spirituality," which is the spirituality of the total, spousal "yes" to the Lord's call.

237. Mary's "yes," given on the day of the Incarnation and kept throughout her life, should be a stimulus and an aid for all women religious and consecrated persons in their total self-giving to the Lord. Each day we should make Mary's "yes" our own, particularly when we say the "great amen" at the end of the Eucharistic Prayer.

May Mary accompany you on your "journey of faith" with her "maternal presence" (*Redemptoris Mater,* 24), in your contemplative, liturgical and community life, in your apostolate and in all the works of mercy which you perform with so much generosity and dedication. Take my affectionate greeting to all the sisters who could not come to this meeting, but who are united with us in spirit. To them and to all the women religious and consecrated persons of Bolivia I impart my apostolic blessing.

17

TO WOMEN RELIGIOUS IN LIMA

May 15, 1988

238. In this, my second visit to Peru, it is a great joy for me to be able to meet you, who belong to different Congregations and Institutes of consecrated life, and whom God loves with a special love. He has asked you for the *total surrender* of your being, soul, body and heart; he has invited you to make of your lives an unmistakable sign of consecration to God; he has summoned you to be witnesses of the fact that earthly realities cannot be transfigured and presented to the Father except in the spirit of the Beatitudes. God has called you to his service, to cooperate, with your active solicitude, in extending the Kingdom of God, the beginning of which is already to be found in the Church (cf. *Lumen Gentium,* 5).

239. Your presence here this afternoon, dear religious, bears witness to your exclusive and irrevocable consecration to Jesus Christ, in the Church, by means of your profession of obedience, chastity and poverty. In this way, you acquire freedom to launch out on this marvelous adventure which is *the total self-giving to the ideals of the Gospel,* to the person of Christ, your Spouse, in the Church, in selfless dedication to serve your neighbor. Yours is not a passing commitment; it is a choice for life, having accepted to be luminous signs of the realities of the Kingdom of God (cf. *Perfectae Caritatis,* 1).

240. Indeed, you are called to be living signs of that Kingdom! Therefore, be light which enlightens, salt which does not lose its taste. The greater your apostolic task, the greater the need to stand out clearly in a world which is confused, since it lacks higher ideals. The more

intensely you are immersed in temporal activities, the more clearly *must you be seen as you are* in your actions: an announcement of the newness of life in Christ. You are called to be signs and, for that reason, to respond to clear and specific demands in the context in which you live! If a sign fades, it loses its *raison d'être,* it is misleading and sows confusion. Only to the extent that, like the Virgin of Nazareth, you renew your "yes" in every instant of your lives, strengthening the commitment made with your vows, in all that it includes, will you be consistent with the identity you have acquired and personally confirmed in the Church. Your "yes" unites itself to the "yes" of Mary. "This *fiat* of Mary—'let it be done to me'—was decisive, on the human level, for the accomplishment of the divine mystery" (*Redemptoris Mater,* 13).

241. How clearly one can see in this Peruvian land the imprint of the generous response of so many women religious and consecrated souls who have worked with self-denial and sacrifice to extend the Kingdom of God! The witness of Rose of Lima, of Ana de los Angeles Monteagudo, and of so many other chosen souls, points out unmistakably the ideal of holiness to which you are called. Given to God in the Lord Jesus, you have a special place in the assembly of the People of God. Your identity is grounded in the new spiritual bond of your religious profession. This is a development of the baptismal bond, which your consecrated lives express and make evident with great intensity (cf. *Perfectae Caritatis,* 5). Through your free and total gift to the Lord, you make yourselves available for the Church's tasks in full fidelity to her teachings and guidelines. Fidelity to the Church without reserve is one of the conditions of your personal gift; to fail in this would be to turn aside from the mission to which you have been called. Indeed, as the Second Vatican Council teaches, "the final norm of the religious life is the following of Christ as it is put before us in the Gospel" (*Perfectae Caritatis,* 2).

242. In your apostolic works of education or assistance with children and young people, with the old and handicapped, when carrying the Word of God through the vast spaces of your land, in helping the young to mature in a human and Christian way, in expressing your affective and effective solidarity with the poor and with those who suffer, you must always take care that you remain totally faithful to *what you are.* Thus, you will offer those whom you serve an ideal which surpasses the goals of a merely human achievement, so as to illumine life itself with the light of faith, which invites us to participate in the riches of God.

243. Those religious who do not perform direct tasks in society also bear witness to the call to transcendence in the midst of the brethren (cf. *Lumen Gentium,* 46; *Gaudium et Spes,* 43). The Pope wants to say to *those dedicated to contemplative life,* that their ecclesial mission continues to have its *raison d'être* in a world full of activity, and that the Church looks with particular predilection upon those who have chosen to give themselves without reserve in cloistered life (cf. *Perfectae Caritatis,* 7; *Ad Gentes,* 18, 40).

244. You, women religious of contemplative life, have made a fundamental choice for the Lord Jesus, leaving everything for his sake, following him, hearing his words, and dedicating yourselves with great care to work tirelessly for the fulfillment of his divine plan (cf. *Perfectae Caritatis,* 5). With complete generosity, you have placed yourselves at the service of the Church. For that reason, you are a treasure of ecclesial life, and at the same time, an effective instrument of apostolate. Always take care to *manifest your communion of mind and heart with the Church.* Be *signs of unity* among yourselves and in the midst of the ecclesial community; by your example, foster the unity of the People of God reconciled in Christ. May your ecclesial service always be one of communion with the local Church and its pastors.

245. Today, the dominant emotion in our hearts is marked by the experience of the intense days of the Eucharistic and Marian Congress which has just ended. They have been days imbued and vivified by faith, by the great mystery of our faith, which, shining ardently in our minds, has illuminated and made clearer the infinite and ineffable love of the God-Man for us; he makes himself food for our earthly pilgrimage and companion on our journey to the Father's house. The words of the liturgy, spoken by the priest after the Eucharistic consecration, "Let us proclaim the mystery of faith," will acquire greater strength from now on when you hear them in your daily Eucharist. Your response will also be even more enthusiastic as you proclaim his victory through the cross and resurrection, and announce always and everywhere his message of salvation, until he comes again.

246. *Faith is the guide and path to communion with God* (cf. Saint John of the Cross, Ascent II 3, 6; *ibid*. II 1, 1). It is the means by which personal encounter with the Lord Jesus is made possible, the breath of the Spirit which enlivens and enlightens the meaning of our lives, the door which opens to filial communication with the Father, because "without faith it is impossible to please (God)" as Scripture tells us (Heb 11:6). The revealed word repeats to us that "the righteous shall live by faith" (Hab 2:4; Rom 1:17; Gal 3:11). How much more should this be said of the religious who has given her whole life to Jesus Christ!

247. You are called to give an ecclesial witness which does not cease to be interested in the world's affairs, but rather throws light on them. Always remember that, when the sense of the sacred seems to evaporate and when the very dimension of faith is questioned by ideologies and materialistic styles of life, *your consecrated life has to be what characterizes you and what distinguishes you*. As my revered predecessor Paul VI wrote: "The world, in spite of the general opinion to the contrary, and although it gives every outward sign of denying God, is in fact seeking God

by strange ways, and is in desperate need of God. This world is looking for preachers of the Gospel to speak to it of God, whom they know as being close to them" (*Evangelii Nuntiandi,* 76).

248. Through your closeness to those most in need, you are particularly conscious of the defects which touch our society and make their sad effects of poverty and injustice felt. Without doubt, you are witnesses of the destitution which afflicts multitudes, wounding them in their dignity as children of God, and witnesses also of the moral decadence which spreads through the body of society like something corrosive. These are clear signs that evangelizing activity needs to be intensified through renewed works of apostolate.

In making plans for the apostolate, one has to start from *a vision of faith* which does not exclude themes such as salvation and configuration to Christ, grace, the Church as mystery, communion and mission, the sacraments, sin as the root of all personal and social evils, commitments in personal and community life, the eternity of the future life, the way of perfection, the acceptance of divine revelation as it is preached and lived in the Church, fidelity to the action of the Holy Spirit: in a word, the authentic religious dimension of the Christian message.

249. There have been cases of pastoral workers who, deeply moved by the sad and unjust state of neglect, the lack of culture, the bodily and human misery of so many of our brothers and sisters, have let their minds be clouded, falling into an unacceptable divorce between the faith they believe and the life they live.

From the very start of the Church, charity has had a preeminent place as a sign and proclamation of the Good News that liberates. Hence, Christians cannot let *the flag of justice,* which is itself a demand of charity, be carried off by any other ideology or system. Love for the poor is a fact which is born of faith, as is shown by the multitude of Christians who over the centuries have followed the Lord in his preferential, non-exclusive love for the poorest, for those on the margin of society, for the sick, the old, and children. As I have pointed out in my recent encyclical on social questions, "The option or love of preference for the poor...is an option or a special form of primacy in the exercise of Christian charity, to which the whole tradition of the Church bears witness. It affects the life of each Christian inasmuch as he or she seeks to imitate the life of Christ, but it applies equally to our social responsibilities" (*Sollicitudo Rei Socialis,* 42).

250. Every Christian and, even more so, every consecrated soul, has to be sensitive to the discovery of each specific person in his human misery. However, that is no reason for efforts made to help resolve the "hunger for bread" to be opposed to those destined to satisfy the "hunger for God." On the contrary, you religious especially should make it clear with your actions that there is an intimate and profound link between the exclusion of God and his salvific plan, and the increase in evils which afflict the human being who separates himself from God. It would be a serious injustice, worse than the first, to forget to announce the Kingdom and neglect to proclaim the Bread of the Word to all!

251. As we have heard in the Gospel reading at the start of this meeting, you are light and salt; your mission is to show the world that you can commit yourselves, as so many of you do, to the sick, the oppressed, children and young people, with a life nourished by the Gospel, without having recourse to outside sources that distort right teaching and dilute Christian life. Aware that you are loved by the Lord, walk the paths of the world proclaiming his love for all, and especially for the poor, the weak, the needy.

252. You will be signs of the evangelical Beatitudes to the extent that you deepen your contemplation of the Word, in intimacy with Christ, and in community life as a

service and gift of self. An intimate relationship with the Lord is, for every Christian and particularly for you religious, like the air that you breathe to stay alive. To deny oneself air is to die. To forget prayer, to let oneself be carried along by routine which chills the affection for the closeness of God, is also to die. There is an intimate link between the life of prayer and the vivifying penetration of the contents of the faith. If prayer is lacking, faith is weakened, and the result is the progressive loss of identity which gives meaning to the evangelical counsels. Let yourselves be loved by God as Father, and, as Saint Teresa of Jesus used to teach, it will be easier "to treat in friendship him whom we know loves us."

253. With regard to the priorities for the religious life in Peru today, I want to draw your attention to the importance nowadays of a correct and suitable *theological, spiritual and human formation.* From the study and meditation of divine revelation, faithful to the teachings of the Magisterium, there will spring forth living waters to flood with Christian meaning your work in hospitals and schools, and of human advancement in the social field.

254. Through you, especially through those who carry out educational activities, I would like to exhort parents to support their sons and daughters when they hear the Lord's call. I wish to ask you, with your own vocation, to help others to see the complete human fulfillment which one obtains following Christ in consecrated life. The Church, as you well know, needs workers dedicated to preaching the Gospel. So, you must all be united in promoting vocations, since the Lord continues to call those whom he wants to participate in his intimate life.

255. Dear religious and people especially consecrated to God, I have wanted to spend this time with you to consider together the beautiful vocation to which, through God's goodness, you have been called; to reflect on the tasks which face you in your apostolic life, and also on the

obstacles which you may come across on your path. The challenge to continue the evangelization of the people of Peru, according to your specific vocation, rises before you. It is a task common to the whole Church, without doubt, but you, by your very condition as women and by the freedom which your virginity gives you, are especially endowed to make a first rate contribution. A woman's heart, with its tenderness and sensibility, is more suited to capturing and joyfully transmitting transcendental values (cf. *Redemptoris Mater,* 46), with firm faith and "hoping against hope" (Rom 4:18). Your consecrated life enables you to give testimony in the Church of the reward promised in the sixth Beatitude: "Blessed are the pure in heart, for they shall see God" (Mt 5:8).

256. May the Virgin Mary be your model, so that it may be said of each of you, as of her: "Blessed is she who believed" (Lk 1:45). May your faith and virginity—as it was with Our Lady—be "a complete openness to the person of Christ, to his whole work, to his whole mission" (*Redemptoris Mater,* 39), so that the world may believe and welcome the salvation which comes from God.

18

LETTER TO ALL CONSECRATED PERSONS BELONGING TO RELIGIOUS COMMUNITIES AND SECULAR INSTITUTES ON THE OCCASION OF THE MARIAN YEAR

May 22, 1988

"Your life is hid with Christ in God" (Col 3:3).

Dear Brothers and Sisters in Christ,

I
INTRODUCTION

257. The Encyclical *Redemptoris Mater* explains the meaning of the Marian Year which the whole Church has been celebrating since last Pentecost and which will continue until the coming Solemnity of the Assumption. In this period, we are seeking to follow the teaching of the Second Vatican Council which, in the Dogmatic Constitution on the Church, designated *the Mother of God* as the one who "precedes" the People of God in the pilgrimage of faith, charity and perfect union with Christ.[1] Because of this fact, *the whole Church finds a perfect "model" in Mary.* What the Council, following the tradition of the Fathers, affirms about the Church as the universal community of the People of God has to be meditated upon by those who together make up this same community, in the light of the vocation of each individual.

258. Certainly many of you, dear brothers and sisters, are trying during the Marian Year to renew your awareness of the link *between the Mother of God and your own specific vocation in the Church.* The present letter which

I am addressing to you as part of this year is meant to help you in your meditations on this subject. In doing so I also wish to refer to the considerations already prepared by the Congregation for Religious and Secular Institutes.[2] At the same time, my purpose in writing is to express *the love which the Church has for you,* for your vocation, for the mission you carry out in the midst of the People of God, in many different places and different ways. All this is a great gift for the Church. Since the Mother of God is constantly present in the life of the Church by reason of the part that she has in the mystery of Christ, your vocation and service are like a reflection of her presence. So we have to ask ourselves what relationship exists between this "model" and the vocation of the consecrated persons who in the various Orders, Congregations and Institutes strive to live their gift of self to Christ.

II
Together with Mary Let Us Meditate upon the Mystery of Our Vocation

259. At the Visitation, Elizabeth, Mary's kinswoman, called her blessed because of her faith: *"And blessed* is she *who believed* that there would be a fulfillment of *what was spoken to her from the Lord"* (Lk 1:45).

The *words* spoken to Mary at the Annunciation were certainly unusual. A careful reading of Luke's text shows that the angel's words to her contain the truth about God, in a manner that already conforms to the Gospel and to the New Covenant. The Virgin of Nazareth has been *introduced into the inscrutable mystery,* which is the living God, the Triune God: Father, Son and Holy Spirit. In that context the Virgin's vocation to be Mother of the Messiah was revealed to her, a vocation to which she responded with her *fiat*: "Let it be done to me according to your word" (Lk 1:38).

Meditating on what happened at the Annunciation, we also think about *our own vocation.* A vocation always marks a sort of turning point on the path of our relationship with the living God. Before each one of you a new perspective has opened up, and a new meaning and dimension have been given to your Christian existence.

260. This happens with a view to the future, to the life that the individual person will live, and to that person's choice and mature decision. The moment of vocation always directly concerns a particular person, but as with the Annunciation at Nazareth it also means a certain "unveiling" of the mystery of God. Before it becomes an accomplished fact within an individual, *before taking on the form of a choice and personal decision, a vocation* refers back to another choice, a choice on the part of God, which has preceded the human choice and decision. Christ spoke of this to the apostles during his farewell discourse: "You did not choose me, but I chose you" (Jn 15:16).

This choice invites us—as it did Mary at the Annunciation—*to discover ourselves in the depths of the eternal mystery of God who is love.* We see that when Christ chooses us, when he says to us "Follow me," then, as the *Letter to the Ephesians* proclaims, "the God and Father of our Lord Jesus Christ" chooses us in him: "He chose us in him before the foundation of the world....He destined us in love to be his sons and daughters...to the praise of his glorious grace which he freely bestowed on us in the Beloved." In addition, "he has made known to us in all wisdom and insight the mystery of his will, according to his purpose which he set forth in Christ" (Eph 1:4-6, 9).

261. These have a universal extension: they speak *of the eternal choice of each and every one in Christ,* of the vocation to holiness which is proper to the adopted children of God. At the same time, they enable us to search the depths of the mystery of each vocation, in particular the vocation which is proper to consecrated persons. In this way each one of you, dear brothers and sisters, is able to realize how deep and supernatural is the reality which we experience when we follow Christ, as he invites us with

the words "Follow me." Then the truth of Saint Paul's words, *"Your life is hid with Christ in God"* (Col 3:3), becomes real and clear for us. Our vocation is hid in the eternal mystery of God before it becomes an accomplished fact within us, before it becomes our human "yes," our choice and decision.

Together with the Virgin at the Annunciation in Nazareth, let us meditate upon the mystery of the vocation which has become our "part" in Christ and in the Church.

III
Together With Mary Let Us Meditate upon the Mystery of Our Consecration

262. Saint Paul writes: *"For you have died, and your life is hid with Christ in God"* (Col 3:3). Let us move from the Annunciation to the Paschal Mystery. The Pauline expression "you have died" corresponds to his words in the *Letter to the Romans,* when he writes about the meaning of the sacrament that makes us part of Christ's life: "Do you not know that all of us who have been baptized into Christ Jesus were baptized into his death?" (Rom 6:3). Thus the expression in the *Letter to the Colossians* "you have died" means that *"we were buried with him by baptism* into death, so that as Christ was raised from the dead by the glory of the Father, we too might walk *in newness of life"* (Rom 6:4).

263. From all eternity God has chosen us in his beloved Son, the Redeemer of the world. Our vocation to the grace of adoption as children of God corresponds to the eternal truth of this being "hid with Christ in God." This vocation for all Christians is realized in time by means of baptism, which buries us in Christ's death. Baptism also marks the beginning of our being "hid with Christ in God"—a reality inscribed in the life story of a particular baptized person. By sharing sacramentally in Christ's redemptive death, we also come to be *united with him* in

his resurrection (cf. Rom 6:5). We share in this total *"newness of life"* (cf. Rom 6:4) initiated in human history by Christ, precisely through his resurrection. This "newness of life" means in the first place being set free from the inheritance of sin, from slavery to sin (cf. Rom 6:1-11).

264. At the same time—and especially—it means *"consecration in the truth"* (cf. Jn 17:17), in which the perspective of union with God—life in God—is fully revealed. This is how our human life is "hid with Christ in God" in a way that is both sacramental and real. To the sacrament there corresponds the living reality of sanctifying grace, which permeates our human life through our sharing in the Trinitarian life of God.

Paul's words, especially in the *Letter to the Romans,* show that all of this "newness of life," which is first shared with us through baptism, includes *the beginning of all the vocations* which during the course of a Christian's life will call for a choice and a conscious decision in the Church. Indeed, every vocation of a baptized person reflects some aspect of that "consecration in the truth" which Christ accomplished by his death and resurrection and made part of his Paschal Mystery: *"For their sake I consecrate myself,* that they also may be consecrated in truth" (Jn 17:19).

265. A person's vocation to consecrate his or her whole life has a special relationship to Christ's own consecration for the sake of mankind. It stems from the sacramental root of baptism, which embraces the first and fundamental consecration of the person to God. Consecration through the profession of the evangelical counsels—through vows or promises—is an organic development of the beginning made at baptism. Consecration includes the mature choice that one makes for God himself, *the spousal response to Christ's love.* When we give ourselves to him in a total and undivided way, we wish "to follow him," making a decision to observe chastity, poverty and obedience in the spirit of the evangelical counsels. We want to be like Christ in the

closest possible way, shaping our lives according to the spirit of the Beatitudes in the Sermon on the Mount. But above all we wish to have charity, which permeates all the elements of the consecrated life and unites them as a true "bond of perfection" (cf. Col 3:14).[3]

266. All of this is included in the Pauline meaning of that "dying" which begins sacramentally at baptism. *It is a dying with Christ which enables us to share in the fruits of his resurrection,* like the grain of wheat which falls to the earth and "dies" for the sake of new life (cf. Jn 12:24). The consecration of a person through sacred bonds determines a "newness of life" which can only be realized on the basis of a "hiddenness" of everything that makes up our earthly life in Christ: our life is hid with Christ in God.

While from a human point of view a person's consecration can be compared to "losing one's life," it is also the most direct way of "finding" it. For Christ says: *"He who loses his life for my sake will find it"* (Mt 10:39). These words certainly express the radical nature of the Gospel. At the same time we cannot fail to notice how much they apply to the human being, and what a unique anthropological dimension they have. What is more fundamental for a human being—man or woman—than precisely this: finding oneself, finding oneself in Christ, since Christ is the "whole fullness" (cf. Col 2:9)?

267. These thoughts concerning the consecration of the person through the profession of the evangelical counsels keep us constantly within the sphere of the Paschal Mystery. *Together with Mary,* let us seek to be *sharers* in this death which brought forth fruits of "new life" in the resurrection: a death like this on the cross was infamous, and it was the death of her own Son! But precisely there, at the foot of the cross, "where she stood, not without a divine plan,"[4] did not Mary realize in a new way everything that she had already heard on the day of the Annunciation? Precisely there, precisely through "the sword which pierced her soul" (cf. Lk 2:35), through an

incomparable "kenosis of faith,"[5] did not *Mary* perceive completely the full *truth about her motherhood?* Precisely there, did she not definitively identify herself with that truth, "rediscovering her soul," the soul which, in the experience of Golgotha, she had to "lose" in the most painful way for the sake of Christ and the Gospel?

It is precisely into this complete "rediscovery" of the truth about her divine motherhood which became Mary's "part" from the moment of the Annunciation that there fit Christ's words on the cross, the words referring to the apostle John, referring to a man: "Behold, your son!" (cf. Jn 19:26).

Dear brothers and sisters: *let us constantly return,* with our vocation, with our consecration, *to the depths of the Paschal Mystery.* Let us present ourselves at Christ's cross next to his Mother. Let us learn our vocation from her. Did not Christ himself say: "Whoever does the will of my Father in heaven is my brother, and sister, and mother" (Mt 12:50)?

IV
Together with Mary Let Us Meditate upon Your Specific Apostolate

268. The events of Easter direct us toward Pentecost, toward the day when "the Spirit of truth comes," to guide "into all the truth" (cf. Jn 16:13) the apostles and the whole Church built on them as her foundation[6] in human history.

Mary brings to the Upper Room at Pentecost the "new motherhood" which became her "part" at the foot of the cross. This motherhood is to remain in her, and at the same time it is to be transferred from her as a "model" to the whole Church, which will be revealed to the world on the day of the descent of the Holy Spirit, the Paraclete. All those gathered in the Upper Room are aware that, from the moment of Christ's return to the Father, their life is hid with him in God. Mary lives in this awareness more than anyone else.

God came into the world and was born of her as the "Son of Man" in order to fulfill the eternal will of the Father who "so loved the world" (cf. Jn 3:16). But through the Word's becoming Emmanuel (God with us), the Father, the Son and the Holy Spirit have also revealed still more profoundly *that the world "abides in God"* (cf. 1 Jn 3:24). "In him we live and move and have our being" (Acts 17:28). God embraces the whole of creation with his creative power, which through Christ has been revealed above all as a power of love. The Incarnation of the Word, the inexpressible and indestructible sign of God's "immanence" in the world, has revealed in a new way his "transcendence." All of this has been already fulfilled and completed in the framework of the Paschal Mystery. The departure of the Son, "the first born of all creation" (Col 1:15), has brought about a new expectation of the one who fills all things: "Because the Spirit of the Lord has filled the world" (Wis 1:7).

269. Those who *together with Mary in the Upper Room in Jerusalem* were awaiting the day of Pentecost have already experienced the "new era." Having received the breath of the Spirit of truth, they are to go out of the Upper Room in order to bear witness, in union with this Spirit, to Christ crucified and risen (cf. Jn 15:26-27). In doing so they are to reveal God who, as love, embraces and fills the world. They must convince everyone that together with Christ they are called to "die" in the power of his death, in order to rise to the life hid with Christ in God.

This is precisely what constitutes *the very core of the Church's apostolic mission.* Coming out of the Upper Room on the day of Pentecost, the apostles initiated the Church, which is wholly apostolic and remains constantly in a state of mission (*in statu missionis*). In this Church each individual receives first in the sacrament of Baptism and then in Confirmation the vocation which, in the words of the Council, is essentially a vocation to the apostolate.[7]

270. The Marian Year began on the Solemnity of Pentecost, so that everyone, together with Mary, might

feel invited to the Upper Room, from which *the entire apostolic history of the Church from generation to generation* takes its beginning. Obviously, dear brothers and sisters, you are among those invited. Under the inspiration of the Holy Spirit you have built your lives and your vocation on the principle of a special consecration, a total self-giving to God. This invitation to the Upper Room at Pentecost means that you must *renew and deepen your awareness of your vocation* in two directions. The first consists in strengthening the apostolate contained in your consecration itself; the second consists in giving new life to the many different apostolic tasks which derive from this consecration in the context of the spirituality and goals of your communities and Institutes, and of each of you individually.

271. *Try to be present with Mary* in the Upper Room at Pentecost. She, more than anyone, will bring you close to this saving vision of the truth about God and man, about God and the world, which is contained in Saint Paul's words: "For you have died, and your life is hid with Christ in God." These words contain the paradox and at the same time the very core of the Gospel message. Dear brothers and sisters, as persons consecrated to God, you have special qualities for bringing people close to this paradox and this Gospel message. You also have the special task of telling everyone—in the mystery of the cross and resurrection—how much the world and the whole of creation are "in God"; how much "we live and move and exist" in him; *how much this God, who is love, embraces everybody and everything;* how much "God's love has been poured into our hearts through the Holy Spirit who has been given to us" (Rom 5:5).

272. Christ has *"chosen you from the world,"* and the world needs your calling, even though at times the world gives the impression of being indifferent to it and of attaching no importance to it. The world needs your being "hid with Christ in God," even though at times it criticizes

the forms of monastic enclosure. For it is precisely through the power of this "hiddenness" that you are able, with the apostles and the whole Church, to make your own the message of our Redeemer's Priestly Prayer: "As you [Father] did send me into the world, *so I have sent them* into the world" (Jn 17:18). You share in this mission, in the apostolic mission of the Church.[8] You share in it in a singular way that is uniquely your own, according to your "own gift" (cf. 1 Cor 7:7). Each one of you, men and women, shares in it, and the more you share in it the more your life "is hid with Christ in God." Herein lies the very source of your apostolate.

273. This fundamental "form" of the apostolate cannot *be hastily changed by being conformed to the mentality of this world* (cf. Rom 12:2). It is true that you often experience the fact that the world loves "its own": "If you were of the world, the world would love its own" (Jn 15:19). But it is Christ who has "chosen you for the world," chosen you so that "the world might be saved through him" (Jn 3:17). Precisely for this reason you cannot abandon your "being hid with Christ in God," since this is an indispensable condition for the world to believe in the saving power of Christ. This "hiddenness," deriving from your consecration, makes each of you a *credible and authentic* person. And this does not close the world to you but on the contrary opens it. Indeed, "the evangelical counsels," as I said to you in my Apostolic Exhortation *Redemptionis Donum,* "in their essential purpose aim at 'the renewal of creation': 'the world,' thanks to them, is to be subjected to man and given to him in such a way that man himself may be perfectly given to God."[9]

Participation in the whole Church's growth in devotion to Mary, as a primary result of the Marian Year, will take different forms and expressions, according to the particular vocation of each Institute, and its fruitfulness will depend on the fidelity of each Institute to its specific gift. Therefore:

274. a) Institutes totally dedicated to *contemplation* "give themselves to God alone in solitude and silence, and through constant prayer and ready penance. No matter how urgent may be the needs of the active apostolate, such communities will always have a distinguished part to play in Christ's Mystical Body," as the Second Vatican Council reminds them.[10]

Thus the Church, looking to Mary in this special year of grace, feels particularly attentive to and respectful of the rich tradition of contemplative life, which men and women, in fidelity to this charism, have successfully established and fostered for the benefit of the ecclesial community and for the good of society as a whole. The Blessed Virgin had a spiritual fruitfulness so intense that it made her the Mother of the Church and of the human race. In silence and in constant attention to the Word of God, and through her intimate union with the Lord, Mary became an instrument of salvation at the side of her divine Son, Christ Jesus. Let all souls consecrated to the contemplative life therefore take comfort, since the Church and the world which she must evangelize receive much light and strength from the Lord thanks to their hidden life of prayer. And following the examples of humility, hiddenness and continual communion with God given by the Handmaid of the Lord, may they grow in love for their vocation as souls dedicated to contemplation.

275. b) All men and women religious who are devoted to the *apostolic life,* to evangelization and to the works of charity and mercy, will find in Mary a model of charity toward God and man. Following this model with generous fidelity, they will respond successfully to the needs of humanity suffering from a lack of certainty, of truth and of a sense of God. It is a humanity that knows the anguish of injustice, discrimination, oppression, wars and hunger. With Mary, religious will share the plight of their brothers and sisters, and help the Church in her readiness to be of service for the salvation of the humanity she meets on her journey today.

276. c) The members of *secular Institutes,* as they live their daily lives within the different strata of society, have in Mary an example and a help in offering the people with whom they share life in the world a sense of the harmony and beauty of a human existence which is all the greater and more joyful the more it is open to God. Members of secular Institutes also offer the testimony of an existence lived in order to build up in goodness communities ever more worthy of the human person. They offer proof that temporal realities, lived with the power of the Gospel, can give life to society, making it freer and more just, for the good of all the children of God, who is Lord of the universe and the Giver of every good thing. This will be the canticle which humanity, like Mary, will be able to raise to God, acknowledging him as almighty and merciful.

277. Through an increased resolve on your part to live your consecration to the full, taking Mary the Mother of Jesus and of the Church as the sublime model of perfect consecration to God, your evangelical witness will grow in effectiveness and lead to a greater fruitfulness of *pastoral work for vocations.*

It is true that a considerable number of Institutes today are experiencing a serious lack of vocations, and in many parts of the world the Church feels the need for more vocations to the consecrated life. In fact the Marian Year may mark a reawakening of vocations through a more trusting recourse to Mary, as to a Mother who provides for her family's needs, and also through a deepened sense of responsibility among all members of the Church for promotion of consecrated life in the Church.

V
Conclusion

278. During the Marian Year all Christians are called to meditate, according to the mind of the Church, *upon the presence of the Virgin Mother of God in the mystery of*

Christ and of the Church.[11] The present letter is meant to be an encouragement to you to meditate upon this presence in your hearts, in the personal history of your soul and your vocation, and at the same time in your religious communities, Orders, Congregations and secular Institutes.

We can truly say that the Marian Year has become *the time for a unique "pilgrimage"* in the footsteps of her who "precedes" the whole People of God in the pilgrimage of faith: she precedes each individual and everyone together. This pilgrimage has many dimensions and contexts: whole nations and even continents are gathering at the Marian shrines, not to mention the fact that individual Christians have their own "interior" shrines, in which Mary is their guide along the path of faith, hope and loving union with Christ.[12]

279. The Orders, Congregations and Institutes, with their experiences, sometimes centuries old, often have their own shrines, *"places" of Mary's presence,* which are linked to their spirituality and even the history of their life and mission in the Church. These "places" recall the particular mysteries of the Virgin Mother, the qualities, the events of her life, the testimonies of the spiritual experiences of the founders or the manifestations of their charism which has then passed to the whole community.

During this year, try to be particularly present in these "places," in these "shrines." Look to them for new strength, for the paths to an authentic renewal of your consecrated life, to the right direction and form for your apostolate. *Seek in them your identity,* like that householder, that wise man, who "brings out of his treasure what is new and what is old" (cf. Mt 13:52).

280. Yes, through Mary seek spiritual vitality, be rejuvenated with her. Pray for vocations. Finally, "do whatever he tells you," as the Virgin said at Cana in Galilee (cf. Jn 2:5). Mary, the Mystical Spouse of the Holy Spirit and our Mother, desires this *from you* and *for you.* Indeed, I exhort you to respond to this desire of Mary's

with a community act of dedication, which is precisely "the response to the love of a Mother."[13]

During this Marian Year, I too with all my heart entrust each one of you and your communities to her, and I bless you in the name of the Father, and of the Son and of the Holy Spirit.

Given in Rome, at Saint Peter's, on May 22, the Solemnity of Pentecost, in the year 1988, the tenth of my Pontificate.

---

1 Cf. *Lumen Gentium*, 58, 63.

2 Cf. *I Religiosi sulle orme di Maria*, Ed. Vaticana, 1987.

3 Cf. *Lumen Gentium*, 44; *Perfectae Caritatis*, 1, 6; *Code of Canon Law* 573, par. 1; 607, par. 710.

4 *Lumen Gentium*, 58.

5 *Redemptoris Mater*, (March 25, 1987), 18; *AAS* 79 (1987), p. 383.

6 Cf. *Lumen Gentium*, 19.

7 Cf. *Apostolican Actuositatem*, 2.

8 Cf. *Code of Canon Law*, 574, par. 2.

9 *Redemptionis Donum* (March 25, 1984), 9; *AAS* 76 (1984), p. 530.

10 *Perfectae Caritatis*, 7.

11 Cf. *Lumen Gentium*, Chapter 8, 52-69.

12 Cf. *ibid.*, 63, 68.

13 *Redemptoris Mater*, 45; *AAS* 79 (1987), p. 423.

19

TO PRIESTS AND RELIGIOUS IN REGGIO EMILIA (ITALY)

June 6, 1988

281. "I have said this to you, that in me you may have peace. In the world you have tribulation; but be of good cheer, I have overcome the world" (Jn 16:33).

Jesus spoke these words of hope to his apostles on the eve of his passion; he repeats these words to you, priests, religious and consecrated persons of this region of Emilia. With the social and economic well-being that is enjoyed in this land, a culture has formed that is often closed—when not outright hostile—to the voice and the values of the spirit. "Be of good cheer," Jesus repeats to you, "I have overcome the world."

282. If Jesus asks your confidence, it is because *he first showed his confidence in you.* He showed his confidence in you when, with an absolutely gratuitous gesture of love, he called you to follow him more closely, to "leave house or brothers or sisters or mother or father or children or lands, for his sake and for the Gospel" (cf. Mk 10:29). He showed his confidence in you when, with a particular outpouring of the Holy Spirit, he consecrated you and, in the diversity of gifts and ministries, he "appointed you that you should go and bear fruit and that your fruit should abide" (Jn 15:16). He showed his confidence in you when he chose you and sent you—you in particular—to be, in this land of Emilia, heralds of his Kingdom, witnesses to his resurrection, a prophetic sign of those "new heavens and new earth in which righteousness will dwell" (2 Pt 3:13).

283. Your mission, like the mission of the whole Church in these last years of the second Christian millen-

nium, is not easy. We find ourselves faced with new situations which, if on the one hand they open up promising and previously unhoped-for possibilities for the proclamation of the Gospel, on the other hand seem to lead people to lose faith in everything in the world that is Christian—indeed, that is human. Yet we must not fear. The mission flowed forth from the Pasch of Jesus; it is the very mission that the Father entrusted to Christ, and that Christ, before ascending into heaven, transmitted to his Church. A mission of salvation, which takes its strength from the presence of Christ and the power of the Spirit.

284. Jesus did not conceal from his apostles *the difficulties of the mission:* the rejection, hostility and persecutions that they would face. "If the world hates you, know that it has hated me before it hated you...Remember the word that I said to you, 'A servant is not greater than his master.' If they persecuted me, they will persecute you" (Jn 15:18, 20). It is not only open persecution that has made and still makes martyrs; there is a more subtle—and thus perhaps more dangerous—snare that is common to many countries in the West. It wishes to make, not martyrs, but "free" men; free—one comes to understand—from every religion and every moral code. This snare does not suffocate the idea of God in blood, but in the accumulation of consumer goods and the satisfaction of natural instincts. It does not combat the idea of Christianity, but ignores it, relegating it to the past as just another myth. Precisely because he foresaw all this, Jesus, before entrusting his mission to the Church, gave us this consoling assurance: "Lo, I am with you always, to the close of the age" (Mt 28:20).

285. This is the certainty that guides and sustains the Church's mission; this is the certainty that must guide and sustain your mission: the certainty that, in Jesus Christ, God is with us; yesterday as today; today as tomorrow, to the end of the world. And "if God is for us, who is against us? Who shall separate us from the love of

Christ? Shall tribulation, or distress, or persecution, or famine, or nakedness, or peril, or the sword?" (Rom 8:31, 35).

This list of obstacles is valid for us, too, though with different connotations. We, too, know the tribulation that comes from being few in number and overburdened with work; we know the feeling of anguish for so many of our brethren who have abandoned the faith; we know today the kind of persecution of which I have spoken. We know hunger: no longer, in this land, hunger for bread, but the hunger for generous souls to follow us; we know nakedness, the emptiness of so many of our houses and so many of our endeavors; we know danger, especially that of infidelity in a world that as a matter of principle refuses stable commitment; we know the sword, the culture of death that seems to have invaded the structures of human society, placing the life of others in danger for motives of profit or ideology, to the point even of destroying life in the mother's womb.

286. What is the answer? Paul's response is precise and resolute: "In all these things we are more than conquerors through him who loved us" (Rom 8:37). Precisely because he loved us, and loves us still, *he is with us*. His is a paschal presence, which not only gives help and comfort, but which gives a new, different and unexpected meaning to the difficulties, the tribulations, the hostilities, the apparent failures. *What might have seemed an obstacle to the mission becomes, in the light of the faith, the secret of its fruitfulness.* The presence of the paschal Christ gives us the certainty that precisely when we seem defeated we are conquerors, indeed "more than conquerors." This is the stupefying logic that has sprung from the cross. On the human plane, the cross of Jesus is a clamorous failure; but precisely from that cross came the unbelievable novelty that has changed the face of life and of human history.

287. Jesus had foretold it: "Unless a grain falls into the earth and dies, it remains alone; but if it dies, it bears

much fruit" (Jn 12:24). It is from the perspective of this parable that Paul was able to exclaim: "For the sake of Christ, then, I am content with weaknesses, insults, hardships, persecutions, and calamities; for when I am weak, then I am strong" (2 Cor 12:10).

Behold the secret of our confidence: when we are weak, then we are strong; the weaker we are, the stronger we are, because we allow the presence and power of the paschal Christ to shine forth all the more clearly. The Church, for 2,000 years already, has journeyed with this paradox, and will continue on...with nothing but this paradox.

288. In entrusting his mission to the Church, Jesus not only assured us of his presence to the end of the world—he promised and transmitted *the power of his Spirit.* The promise, which was echoed various times during his farewell discourse, found its first fulfillment in the Upper Room, on the very evening of Easter. "Jesus came and stood among them. He said to them, 'Peace be with you. As the Father has sent me, even so I send you.' And when he had said this, he breathed on them, and said to them, 'Receive the Holy Spirit'" (Jn 20:19-23). The complete fulfillment of the promise took place on the day of Pentecost, when "there appeared to them tongues as of fire, distributed and resting on each one of them. And they were all filled with the Holy Spirit..." (Acts 2:3-4).

289. From that time forward *the Holy Spirit has been working* in the life and history of mankind. He is at work in the world, which is approaching the third Christian millennium, in order to make it the Kingdom of love of the Father. He is at work in the Church, in this Church of the Second Vatican Council, which, in the continuity of the Christian tradition, is renewing herself from day to day in order to be ever closer to God and man. He is at work in your Churches, in these courageous Churches of Emilia, which, in a particularly difficult pastoral situation, are rediscovering their essential vocation: the proclamation

of the Gospel here, today, to all the people and in all the situations in which they live and work. He is at work in your communities, even if they are little and poor, so that, precisely because they are little and poor, they may be rich in faith and great in charity.

290. The Spirit of God is the Spirit of life, who is capable of causing life to burst forth even where everything seemed dead and withered (cf. Ezek 37). That is why we can and must have confidence. Not only can we, but we must. For Christians, and much more for the consecrated, hope is not a luxury, it is a duty. To hope is not to dream; on the contrary, it is to allow oneself to be taken hold of by him who can transform dreams into reality.

291. Yet hope, if it is not to fade, must be *nourished by an intense life of prayer,* of listening to the Word of God, of contemplation. The increase of work to be done in the Lord's vineyard just as the number of laborers is diminishing can make us forget that we have been called first of all to remain with the Lord, to listen to his Word, to contemplate his face. The contemplative dimension is inseparable from the mission, because, according to the famous definition of Saint Thomas, a definition also cited by the Council, the mission is essentially *"contemplata aliis tradere" (Summa Theol.* II-II, q. 188, a. 7; cf. *Presbyterorum Ordinis*, 13), the transmission to others of what we have already contemplated at length.

292. Whence the need for long periods of prayer, of concentration, of adoration; the need for the assiduous and meditative reading of the Word of God; the need for a contemplative rhythm—thus calm and restful—in the celebration of the Eucharist and of the Liturgy of the Hours; the need for silence as the indispensable condition for realizing a deep communion with God and making of our whole lives a prayer. As consecrated persons we must not only pray, we must *be a living prayer.* We might go further and say that we must pray without seeming to. We

must pray even when we do not seem to have the time, but we must pray. Another paradox. Humanly speaking, it is impossible: how can one pray without being at prayer? However, if Saint Paul tells us that "the Holy Spirit prays in us," then that is something else again....

293. *The model of our hope is the Mother of God.* Like Abraham, and more than Abraham, Mary "had faith, hoping against all hope" (cf. Rom 4:18) and abandoned herself trustingly to the Word of the living God and the power of his Spirit.

On this day of grace, in this marvelous church that the piety of the people of Reggio Emilia has built to the Madonna della Ghiara, we turn to her and ask of her the courage to remain with her near the cross and to accept the logic of the cross; the courage to cry out with the strength of the Spirit: "We are treated as impostors, and yet are true; as unknown, and yet well known; as dying, and behold, we live; as punished, and yet not killed; as sorrowful, yet always rejoicing; as poor, yet making many rich; as having nothing, and yet possessing everything" (2 Cor 6:8-10).

Holy Mary, Mother of God, Mother of blessed hope, pray for us.

20

TO PRIESTS, RELIGIOUS AND SEMINARIANS IN PARMA (ITALY)

June 7, 1988

294. "You are the salt of the earth...You are the light of the world" (Mt 5:13-14).

Dear brothers and sisters, these words of Christ are addressed in a *special and eminent* way to you, priests, religious, and seminarians.

The symbol of light refers to the *truth*. A special aspect of the priestly and religious vocation is precisely that of an *exemplary love for the truth*. If every Christian should be "consecrated in the truth" (cf. Jn 17:17), you must be so in a special way, since by divine mandate you are guides and light for the People of God, who rightfully expect help from you to understand better the Gospel and the truth about Christ. You are also guides and light for every person, because everyone has in his heart a thirst for the truth, even if he does not know Christ.

295. Also, the symbol of the salt is obvious. That is, your speech, your witness, must *"give a flavor" to the life of this world,* make known the profound and ultimate meaning of creation and bring it God's light.

Therefore, in a special way your vocation is *to know how to savor,* and *be like experts* in, the divine realities. You are thus led to give a supernatural "flavor" to the realities of this world. This means that you must be, in an exemplary fashion, *disciples of wisdom,* understood not merely as human knowledge, but also and above all as *a gift of the Holy Spirit.*

296. Never forget this responsibility which is yours. If food is tasteless, it is always possible to flavor it with salt. However, if the salt itself is tasteless, as Jesus

remarks, "how shall its saltiness be restored?" (Mt 5:13). If the wisdom of the Holy Spirit is lacking, nothing can replace it. You are called in a special way to taste this wisdom and make it attractive to mankind.

297. Notwithstanding your poverty, you are called to enrich the world. How shall this be possible? By imitating the prophet Elijah from what we have heard in the first reading of today's Mass.

In him we notice two qualities which he had very clearly and which made him great: knowledge of his *human limitations* and awareness of the *divine power* to which he was totally committed and of whom, as a prophet, he wished to be the instrument and spokesman.

298. Dear brothers and sisters, among the People of God you also are called in a special way to this double awareness, to this wisdom and this prophetic spirit, which speaks in God's name; it announces God's Word to everyone, and with preferential love, to the poor and humble. Even in the desert, which, as with Elijah, seems to remove all hope—I refer to the absence and coldness of many, and to the lack of vocations—you also must trust in the power of God's word on which your word, your testimony, is based; thus you shall prepare for the triumph of good.

299. May the Blessed Virgin Mary, who has profoundly lived this law of Christian hope near the cross of her Son, obtain for us the *spirit of prophecy,* to make us successfully overcome present difficulties and look serenely towards the future.

Praised be Jesus Christ!

21

TO THE WORLD CONGRESS OF SECULAR INSTITUTES AT CASTEL GANDOLFO

August 26, 1988

300. With great joy I welcome you on the occasion of your fourth World Congress, and I thank you for your presence in such great numbers. You are the distinguished representatives of an ecclesial reality which, especially in this century, is a sign of a special "movement" of the Holy Spirit in the heart of God's Church. In fact, the secular Institutes have clearly stressed the value of the consecrated life for those who work "in the world," that is, for those who are involved in secular activities, whether as diocesan priests, or especially, as lay persons. For the laity, in fact, the story of the secular Institutes marks an important stage in the development of the doctrine concerning the special nature of the lay apostolate and in the recognition of the laity's universal call by Christ to holiness and service.

Your mission today is situated in the perspective of a reaffirmed theological tradition, that of the "consecratio mundi," that is, in restoring all things in Christ as the sole Head (cf. Eph 1:10), working from within, in secular life.

301. I am pleased with the theme chosen for the present assembly: "The mission of the secular Institutes in the world of 2000." In fact, this is a complex subject which corresponds to the Church's short-term hopes and expectations.

This program is extremely challenging for you, because it opens up the horizons of the Third Millennium to your specific vocation and spiritual experience. It does so in order to help you to become more and more aware of your call to holiness while living in the world, and to collaborate in the work of salvation and evangelization of the whole People of God through your consecration, interiorly and authentically lived. (...)

302. The impact of the Third Millennium of the Christian era is doubtless stimulating for all who intend to dedicate their lives to the good and progress of humanity. All of us would wish that the new era would correspond to the plan which the Creator has designed for humanity. It is he who makes and develops history, as the story of salvation for people of every epoch. Therefore, in the new millennium, each person is called to a commitment to making a new chapter in the history of the redemption.

You intend to contribute to the sanctification of the world from within, "in saeculo viventes," working in the midst of the world, "praesertim ad intus," according to the law of the Church (*Code of Canon Law,* can. 710).

Although in the *secular* state, you are *consecrated.* From this comes the originality of your task: you are fully *laity*, but you are consecrated; you are bound to Christ by a special vocation, to follow him more closely, to imitate his condition as "Servant of God," in the humble profession of chastity, poverty and obedience.

303. You are aware of sharing with all people the dignity of being God's children, Christ's living members, incorporated into the Church, invested through baptism with the common priesthood of the faithful. However, you have also accepted the message intrinsically connected with this dignity: that of the commitment to holiness, to the perfection of love; that of answering the call of the evangelical counsels which consists of a gift of self to God and to Christ with an undivided heart and total abandonment to the will and guidance of the Spirit. You fulfill this commitment, not by being separated from the world, but from within the complex situations of work, culture, the professions, and social services of every kind. This means that your professional activities and the condition of sharing earthly cares with other lay persons will be the sphere of trials, challenges, the cross; but also of the call,

the mission, and the moment of grace and of communion with Christ, in which your spirituality is built up and developed.

304. As you well know, this requires a continual spiritual progress in your behavior as regards people, the present situation, and history. You are required, both in the small and major events of the world, to be able to show *a presence,* that of Christ, who always walks beside people, even when these ignore and deny him. This also requires permanent attention to the salvific importance of the events of daily life, so that they can be interpreted in the light of faith and Christian principles.

Therefore, this demands of you a deep union with the Church, fidelity to its ministry, a loving, total adherence to its thought and message, in full awareness that this attitude comes from the special bond which unites you to the Church.

305. This does not mean a lessening of the legitimate autonomy of the laity as regards the consecration of the world; rather it is a question of placing it in its proper light, so that it is not weakened, and does not operate in isolation. The dynamism of your mission, as you see it, far from distancing itself from the Church's life, is realized in a union of love with it.

306. Another fundamental requirement consists in the generous and conscious acceptance of the mystery of the cross. Every ecclesial action is objectively rooted in the work of salvation, in Christ's redemptive action. It draws its strength from the sacrifice of the Lord, from his blood shed upon the cross. Christ's sacrifice, ever present in the work of the Church, constitutes her strength and her hope, her most mysterious and greatest gift of grace. The Church well knows that her history is one of abnegation and immolation.

307. Your situation as consecrated laity makes you verify each day how true this is in the area of the activities and mission that each of you also accomplishes. You know what dedication the work of struggling against self, the world and its evil desires involves. Yet, it is the only way to achieve that true interior peace which only Christ can and does give.

This evangelical way, precisely because it is often traveled in conditions of solitude and suffering, is the way which gives you hope, because, in the cross, you are sure to be in communion with our Redeemer and Lord.

308. Let the cross not discourage you. It will be a help and a support to you in extending the work of redemption and in bringing Christ's sanctifying presence to others. Such an attitude on your part will show the provident action of the Holy Spirit, who "blows where he wills" (Jn 3:8). Only he can enkindle the strength, initiative and powerful signs through which Christ's work is brought to completion.

309. The task of spreading the gift of the Redemption to all human activity is the mission which the Spirit has given to you. It is a sublime mission, demanding courage, yet it is always a motive of happiness for you, if you live in the communion of charity with Christ and with others.

The Church of the year 2000 expects from you a worthwhile collaboration along the difficult journey of the world's sanctification. (...)

22

TO WOMEN RELIGIOUS IN TURIN (ITALY)

September 4, 1988

310. I am happy to meet you on the occasion of these celebrations in honor of Saint John Bosco on the centenary of his death.

Your very presence here, in the little town of Valdocco, is itself an eloquent discourse!

In the variety of your charisms and vocations you are a splendid image of the Church, enriched by the Spirit of the Lord with so many gifts and ministries to serve humanity according to the Gospel.

"The Church expresses to you her gratitude for your consecration and for your profession of the evangelical counsels, which are a particular *testimony of love*" (Redemptionis Donum, 14).

Indeed, throughout the centuries, this testimony has never been interrupted, but on the contrary, it has grown ever more luminous.

Don Bosco, that man who was gifted with a keen sense of spiritual discernment, was deeply aware of it; he always valued the contribution of women, and in particular that of consecrated women, in the building up of a more human and more Christian society. It was no accident that, from the very beginning, he associated his mother Margherita to his work as an educator, and he later involved an ever growing number of women from every social class in his intense apostolic activity. He founded a women's Congregation, welcoming the original and creative contribution of many women, especially that of Saint Maria Domenica Mazzarello.

311. Don Bosco, disciple of Christ, gave witness throughout his life to the primacy of the interior life. He

marvelously combined this primacy with intense activity for others, a generous and joyous service, both tireless and radical, which allowed his communion with the Lord to shine through.

Religious life always maintains this primacy, and you can offer a precious contribution in this sense, by seeking and offering a new feminine identity through your being, which in turn is reflected in your actions.

"Through your being," because by the profession of the evangelical counsels, all too often presented solely as renunciation, you positively and joyfully indicate where the absolute of the human person lies, and you refute the idolatry of the society of possessions, of the empirical and the contingent.

By your profession of the evangelical counsels you prophetically announce the future good, thus indicating the origin, the meaning and the definitive goal of human destiny.

From the viewpoint of this eschatological horizon you have much to say, particularly to the women of today, as a response to the emerging situations of the present socio-cultural context.

312. The first response concerns the many and complex questions about the meaning of religious life today. The secularized society makes no reference to the transcendent, can no longer value the richness of a life lived within the walls of a convent, does not understand the renunciation of the joy of one's own family in view of a deeper and broader motherhood, the choice of a love that does not disappoint, the meaning of an authentic femininity found in a virginity which is viewed as a way to a loftier realization.

In this society in which there is "an invading theoretical and pragmatic materialism which closes the horizons of the spirit and of the transcendent...you are called to sustain the civilization of love and of life, to be the soul of the Christian leaven, the guides within the horizons of the faith.... In the Church you incarnate the task of Mary. You have an irreplaceable role, especially in the specific areas that correspond to your charisms and your sensitivities."[1]

313. In the contemporary world you are called to show forth with crystal clarity invisible values that are real and can be lived by all.

You have inherited a rich tradition: often in the past, it was precisely through consecrated women that a new feminine identity was proposed, which, like a prophecy, responded to the questions and appeals of the world around them.

Turin and this diocese have always been a fertile source of generous and creative women coming from all social classes. They served and still serve, with evangelical spirit, those who are in need, as well as those who are sometimes forgotten and despised.

The response, then, comes from you, from your being, from your profession of the evangelical counsels, from our apostolic activity. "The world needs the authentic 'contradiction' provided by religious consecration as an unceasing stimulus of salvific renewal" (*Redemptionis Donum,* 14). And experience teaches that no movement of the religious life has any value if it is not simultaneously a movement towards the interior, towards the depth of being, where Christ has his dwelling.

314. In the course of history, many ideological proposals which regarded progress and personal fulfillment as sexual license, elimination of moral laws, and emancipation from religion, have contradicted one another. The identity crisis of persons and institutions is a sad sign of this and becomes a pressing cry for help.

Christian revelation offers the salvific response that is born of the truth about humanity, from an anthropology that is linked to the divine.

Indeed, in proclaiming the truth about the human person, it makes its specific contribution in confirming the perfect equality of man and woman as the image of God and his interlocutors. Man and woman, in that they are the image of God, make visible in the universe the unity of God who lives not in solitude but in communion: the one and triune God. In establishing the Kingdom of God, Jesus goes back to this original communion so that "there is neither Jew nor Greek, there is neither slave nor free person, there is not male and female; for you are all one in Christ Jesus" (Gal 3:28).

315. Particularly in regard to woman, Jesus showed himself as Liberator and Savior. He frees her from the desire for possession and the dominion of man (Mt 5:28), overturns the mentality of the age which also affects his disciples, a mentality that seeks to perpetuate overbearing relationships (cf. Mt 19:3-10). He declares her exempt from legal impurity precisely by his behavior. He refuses to identify her role with biological motherhood and reveals her dignity in the faith in a new type of relationship. He proposes her as a model of faith and love. It is by means of the woman whose sins had been pardoned that he announces the specific nature of the Gospel message: love without limits (cf. Lk 7:47, 50); he points out the generous gift of the widow who, in offering her mite for the Temple, was giving all that she had (cf. Lk 21:1-4). On the lips of a woman John places one of the most beautiful professions of faith (cf. Jn 11:27).

The women followed Jesus spontaneously and they became heralds of the messianic announcement (cf. Jn 4:28,30; Mt 28:1-8).

Among all of them a singular and unique place belongs to Mary, the Mother of Jesus, who synthesizes the Israel of God through her unreserved "yes," her charity without limits, through her maternity in relationship to the disciples of Jesus for all times.

316. The Church, fruit of Christ's salvific work and the place in which he continues to save every person, is presented as overcoming all dialectical argument when she is understood in her profound constitutive mystery. Indeed, she was described by the Council as "a kind of

sacrament or sign of intimate union with God, and of the unity of all mankind. She is also an instrument for the achievement of such union and unity" (*Lumen Gentium,* 1).

May you, dearest Sisters, be witnesses to this Church, to this mystery in life and word, as was Blessed Anna Michelotto, who was a tireless promoter of the Gospel message here in Turin, in every social class, but most of all among the poor and the infirm. Like her, you also give your precious testimony announcing the primacy of the Absolute, of the one and triune God who wishes to enter into conversation with us. Show that, for the believer, communion with the One who is transcendent, equally expressed in the solitude of prayer, cannot be an escape or withdrawal from the company of one's brothers and sisters. As in Mary and in the Church, so also the women of today should be able to discover in your life a very concrete and unique adventure, lived not in an individualistic or self-centered way, but in solidarity with the whole of human history and all of creation.

317. This is the message which you can proclaim today in the Church and in society. The message is a timely one, an urgent one, and is meant to emphasize that the solution to problems must be sought in a wider and therefore more human framework of values, which gives the primacy to the person as the subject of communion. It must overcome revindications, the absolutization of roles, the opposition of rights, all expressions which are still a sign of sin and not of freedom.

The Gospel marks out the road of liberation that is beyond the expectation of our human means: Jesus proposes new types of relationships that are not under the power of sin or of "hardness of heart," but under God's merciful and paternal lordship which celebrates the victory of charity without limits. Thus is born a new bond of relationship, not founded on flesh and blood, but on faith, which is expressed in fruitful and profound communion, which transcends biological and earthly dimensions.

Mary, the Mother of Jesus and of the Church, is the prototype of it; your consecration is a prophecy of it extended in time.

318. Now, here is a task for you: be signs of this new type of relations, of this new bond of relationship, not in an abstract manner, but in the concrete fabric of your existence, as a progressive discovery of the way to be disciples of Jesus in every moment and condition of life.

May the Spirit of the Lord, and Mary's motherly protection guide you in this marvelous adventure to bring about the civilization of love and of life. With your Gospel witness you should be like leaven on this human and Christian journey.

Thus your existence becomes a mission, and it could not be otherwise, because this is the structure of the believer according to the Gospel.

Your coming here to the sanctuary of Mary Help of Christians, in memory of Don Bosco, is an invitation to reflect profoundly on your "being" in order to draw from it, with courage, the consequences for action.

In the letter addressed to the Rector Major of the Salesian Society I treated some of these consequences which are an appeal especially to you, who are committed to many apostolic works: the Church "in this period so close to the year 2000, ...feels invited by her Lord to look upon (youth) with a special love and hope, and to consider their education as one of her primary pastoral responsibilities" (*Juvenum Patris, 1).*[2]

319. I would therefore like to call your attention to your responsibility, particularly for the young generations, according to your particular charism and your commitment to education.

Your prophecy, your evangelical life, the expression of the new bond of relationship, is most of all an announcement for them, who are the future of society and of the Church.

Today still, more than yesterday, you can and should

let the beauty of a life spent entirely for the Lord in service of one's brothers and sisters shine before the eyes of youth.

Through your chastity you announce to young people the beauty of the love of the human heart made fruitful by the Gospel; you announce the future resurrection and eternal life, that life in union with God, that love which contains in itself and completely pervades all the other loves of the human heart, that liberation brought by Jesus for all (cf. *Redemptionis Donum,* 11).

320. In her *Magnificat,* which has become the Canticle of the Church and of humanity which yearns for salvation, Mary has proclaimed this human and feminine liberation: she "is the most perfect image of freedom and of the liberation of humanity and of the universe" (*Redemptoris Mater*, 37).

321. May she, who in her own life gave us an "example of that maternal love by which all should be fittingly animated who cooperate in the apostolic mission of the Church on behalf of the rebirth of humanity" (*Lumen Gentium,* 65), teach you, and guide you in the evangelical motherhood proper to your vocation.

She continues through the centuries to be a maternal presence as is shown by Christ's words: "Woman, behold your Son"; "Behold your Mother" (cf. Jn 16:26 ff).

"Never take your gaze off Mary; listen to her when she says: 'Do what Jesus tells you' (Jn 2:5). Pray to her too with daily solicitude, that the Lord may continue to raise up generous souls who can say 'yes' to his vocational call.

322. "To her I entrust you, and with you the whole world of youth, that being attracted, animated and guided by her, they may be able to attain through the mediation of your educative work the stature of 'new men' for a new world: the world of Christ, Master and Lord" (*Juvenum Patris,* 20). I confide you to Mary, the New Woman, Mother of the Church, of the new humanity. May she inspire you in the discovery of a new feminine identity

according to the Gospel. By her powerful intercession may she make all of your initiatives fruitful and assist you with her maternal protection. With this wish I bless you with all my heart.

[1] Cf. *Discourse to priests, religious and committed laity* in Florence, October 18, 1985. *L'Osservatore Romano,* English language edition, November 17, 1986, p. 4.

[2] *Juvenum Patris,* Letter of the Supreme Pontiff John Paul II to Rev. Egidio Vigano, Rector Major of the Society of St. Francis de Sales, on the occasion of the centenary of the death of Saint John Bosco, January 31, 1988. Cf. *L'Osservatore Romano,* No. 6, English language edition, February 8, 1988.

23

TO PRIESTS, RELIGIOUS AND SEMINARIANS IN BULAWAYO (ZIMBABWE)

September 12, 1988

323. I greet you with the words of Saint Paul: "I am so proud of you that...I am filled with consolation and my joy is overflowing" (2 Cor 7:4).

This is indeed a moment of great joy for me, to meet you, the priests, the men and women religious, and the seminarians of Zimbabwe. In each one of you I see the great mystery of God's love. To you the Lord has spoken as in the book of Leviticus: "Be consecrated to me, because I, the Lord, am holy and I will set you apart from all these peoples so that you may be mine" (20:26). Your lives are rooted in that divine call and your confidence is in the One who sustains your ministry and witness. "His faithful love endures forever" (Ps 118:1).

Here, in Saint Mary's Cathedral in Bulawayo, with the west window over the altar depicting the Immaculate Conception and scenes from the life of the Mother of God, I wish to share these moments with you *in the spirit of Mary's song of praise:* "Holy is his name, and his mercy reaches from age to age" (Lk 1:49-50).

324. Brother *priests:* the theme of my visit to Zimbabwe is also the challenge of your priestly ministry: "coming together in Christ," coming together in the Christian community, through reconciliation. It is your task to build up your parishes and each local Church in fidelity to the *Word of God,* above all by breaking the *Bread of life* for your people and by involving them in *works of faith and service* (cf. Acts 2:42).

In order to do this, you yourselves are first called to intimate union with the Lord. You must be men of God, accustomed to prayer and self-giving, humble of heart yet courageous in proclaiming the word "in season and out of season" (cf. 2 Tim 4:2). You must be true spiritual fathers and guides of your people. You must be brothers to each other in every difficulty.

325. One of the outstanding characteristics of African people is that they cherish family relationships. Accordingly, in this cultural context the Church must appear ever more clearly as *the family of God's beloved children.* Exactly a year ago, during my visit to the United States, I spoke of the parish as the "family of families," "our family in the Church...in which there are no strangers or aliens" (*Address at Our Lady of Guadalupe Plaza,* San Antonio, September 13, 1987). It is your task, my brothers, to instill this family spirit into your parishes and small Christian communities, by being yourselves a reflection of God's fatherly love for his people.

326. The *presbyterium* too should be a family of many brothers under the bishop, "co-workers in the same undertaking" (*Presbyterorum Ordinis,* 8). Occasions to pray together, study together and share the experiences of your priestly life and work are a necessary part of your lives. How beautiful when you welcome one another into your houses with the peace of Christ in your hearts! How important it is that you support each other through prayer, and with helpful advice and discernment!

327. The renewal in ecclesial life which the Second Vatican Council advocated has certainly, in spite of difficulties and some misunderstandings, produced abundant spiritual fruits in the life of the Church. This renewal has to be clearly evident in the ministry of priests who are called to guide and animate it. Among the more important gifts which the Holy Spirit has bestowed on the Church through the Council is the greater awareness of *the universal call to holiness of life.* Your ministry cannot be understood apart from your own sharing in the divine life, apart from prayer and penance, apart from self-giving,

charity and justice. And the fruit of your ministry is to foster these things in the lives of your people. Indeed, you find nourishment for your own spiritual life in pastoral leadership and activity (cf. *Presbyterorum Ordinis*, 14).

328. Under the guidance of the Council, the laity are acquiring a more precise understanding of their baptismal grace and their role in the priestly People of God. They show an ever greater thirst for God's Word and they look to the Church's spiritual, theological and social doctrine to enlighten them in their everyday lives. Many of them yearn for a more responsible role in parish life, in liturgical activities, in catechesis and in service to those in need. In all of this *your spiritual leadership* is tested. Your proclamation of the Word of God must provide them with ever more solid spiritual nourishment; it should be the result of your own study and prayerful meditation. Your teaching must clearly reflect the Church's response to the increasingly complex questions raised by modern life. In Saint Matthew's Gospel, Isaiah's description of the Suffering Servant is applied to Jesus, and it can be applied to each one of you:

> "I will endow him with my spirit, and he will proclaim the true faith to the nations... He will not break the crushed reed, nor put out the smouldering wick till he has led the truth to victory" (Mt 12:18-20).

329. As the people of Zimbabwe and of the whole of Southern Africa strive for *reconciliation and brotherhood,* I pray that you as priests will exercise the special charism of being able to reconcile your people and "bring them together in Christ." You well know that before there can be genuine and lasting reconciliation there has to be *a conversion,* that change of heart which is brought about by willing acceptance of its real consequences in personal and social life.

The ministry of reconciliation is above all a struggle against sin and evil. In administering the *sacrament of*

Penance, you are entrusted with the spiritual power to loose and bind. If you yourselves appreciate the blessings of this sacrament, you will be better able to convey this deep appreciation to the faithful, who nowadays often need more personal attention and more patient listening on the part of the confessor. In each country I visit I appeal to the priests to make themselves as available as possible to those who wish to be freed from sin and renewed in grace, to be reconciled with the Lord and with the Church. And I make this same appeal to you: love this sacrament and receive it often.

330. My brother priests, the presence of God's Kingdom in Zimbabwe makes itself felt especially through the power and truth of your ministry, centered on the Eucharist. Therefore, I earnestly encourage you to be ever more conformed to Christ, and to draw the spiritual resources you need for "shouldering the sacred task of the Gospel" (*Presbyterorum Ordinis,* 2) from your daily sharing in Christ's Paschal Mystery. May you always cherish Mary as the Mother of your vocation and the perfect example of discipleship and service.

331. *Men and women religious of Zimbabwe!* You too are bound to Christ by a unique relationship. You have received a special sharing in Christ's consecration of himself to the Father for the sake of mankind (cf. Jn 17:19). It is a consecration which he fulfilled through his death and resurrection and which you realize in a specific way by fulfilling his words: "He who loses his life for my sake will find it" (Mt 10:39).

In a letter to all consecrated persons which I wrote during the recently completed Marian Year, I sought to emphasize something which is at the heart of religious life, namely, the positive significance of dying with Christ in order to share in his resurrection. I said that what is fundamental for a human being—man or woman—is precisely this: "finding oneself in Christ, since Christ is the 'whole fullness' (cf. Col 2:9)" (Letter of May 22, 1988,

III). To the extent that you "find yourselves in Christ," the maturity of your faith and charity will make you his prophetic witnesses in each local Church and before the world. In this way you will effectively proclaim the eternal value of Christ's saving message.

332. It is your special calling to bear public witness, through your way of life, to the "newness of life" which the Incarnate Son of God introduced into human affairs (cf. Rom 6:4). You bear this witness in the concrete historical circumstances of present-day Zimbabwe and contemporary Africa, which have an urgent need for a renewed humanism, expressed in *a culture which defends life and promotes human solidarity,* to be built on the best traditions of this continent in dialogue with the perennial and universal truths revealed in Jesus Christ.

333. Your religious consecration, manifested through the observance of the evangelical counsels of chastity, poverty and obedience and made fruitful in the many activities of your religious Institutes, *is inseparable from the Church's evangelizing and sanctifying mission.* Your consecration will have little sense without a profound love of the Church as God's chosen instrument for the salvation of mankind. Jesus says: "I have come so that they may have life and have it to the full" (Jn 10:10). All of us, the Successor of Peter and each one of you, must consider ourselves in the first place as apostles sent to proclaim the "life" which God offers in Christ Jesus. To reduce the "Good News" to anything less would be to diminish the very potential for transformation which the Spirit generates in the Church and of which your consecrated life is a clear witness and powerful instrument.

334. Religious life is the countersign to those tendencies towards selfish and excessive individualism, towards greed and ruthless competition which are among the factors that hinder authentic human development here in Africa and elsewhere. Religious life educates you to be

especially sensitive to the needs of the poor, the disadvantaged, the sick and the handicapped, and of those left behind by progress. In your service to others in towns or rural areas, in hospitals and schools, in social services and charitable activities, you are not just serving the material development of your people, *you are also upholding their human dignity.* You treat others as God's sons and daughters, made in his likeness. You serve them as Christ's beloved brothers and sisters.

335. Here, I would like you to reflect on the fact that certain well-tried forms of apostolate, such as education and health care, are a most effective way of defending and promoting human rights because they defend the human person from the basic indignity of ignorance and abandonment. I wish to encourage you, especially the religious sisters, to persevere in these endeavors in fidelity to the charisms which the Holy Spirit has bestowed on your Institutes.

My dear sisters: as consecrated women you have a most profound effect on the way *the Gospel is incorporated into local culture.* Very often you "vivify" a Christian community from its very roots, stimulating and accompanying its growth in a way that is not open to others. The work of the first courageous women religious in this region has left an indelible mark on the Church here.

336. Let us praise God together for the selfless service of the many expatriate sisters who have brought untold blessings upon the Church in this land. Theirs is a significant testimony of the universality of Christian love. And the Zimbabwean-born sisters are the blossoming forth of the divine gift which the Church in this land has received from her Lord: "like branches sprouting out wondrously and abundantly (they) form a tree growing in the field of the Lord from a seed divinely planted" (*Lumen Gentium,* 43). This particular seed was planted almost a hundred years ago, when after a long and hazardous journey the first Dominican sisters entered this area, and it has not ceased to give the finest fruits ever since.

337. I wish to say a special word of encouragement to the Poor Clares who have established a community in Harare, the first of its kind in Zimbabwe. *The contemplative life is an integral part of the life of every particular Church.* The presence of these sisters is a sign of a maturing community of faith, and they deserve the respect and love due to their special vocation. I pray that there may be many Zimbabwean vocations to the contemplative life, which the Council calls "the glory of the Church and an overflowing fountain of heavenly graces" (*Perfectae Caritatis,* 7).

338. Dear religious brothers: your faithfulness and prayerfulness are of vital importance to the Church, and the service you render is indispensable. Your example as conscientious administrators, technical instructors and skilled artisans, demonstrating the dignity of work, is of immense value to a developing country which cannot progress unless it holds workers in high esteem. The example of your joyous following of Christ and your industrious pastoral service is a source of encouragement for many. I invite the Church in Zimbabwe to promote vocations to the brotherhood without any fear that this will divert vocations from the priesthood, for it is the Lord who calls where and when he wishes.

339. I also offer a special greeting to all *the seminarians* and candidates to religious life in Zimbabwe. Always give thanks to God who gives you this opportunity to discern in faith and trust *the calling which is the reason for your special place in the Church.* Remember, it is a call to service and holiness of life. It means detachment from material things, and the practice of all the Christian virtues, especially chastity, love of neighbor and zeal for the salvation of souls. Place your trust in the Lord: *he is your Shepherd, he guides you along the right path; he is true to his name* (cf. Ps 22 [23]:1,3).

340. Dear priests and religious: the cost of discipleship is never small. Here in Bulawayo, I recall the memory

of the first bishop of this diocese, Adolph Schmitt, and of the other priests, religious sisters and brothers, and lay people who lost their lives in the difficult years of the struggle for independence, or as the result of more recent acts of violent aggression. May their sacrifice inspire the entire Church in this land to "press forward amid the persecutions of the world and the consolations of God, announcing the cross and resurrection of the Lord until he comes" (*Lumen Gentium,* 8). I entrust you all to Our Lady, Queen of Peace, whose shrine nearby is a reminder that true peace comes as a gift from the heart of our loving God.

May the peace of Christ be with you all!

24

TO PRIESTS, RELIGIOUS AND LAITY IN GABORONE (BOTSWANA)

September 13, 1988

341. It is a great joy for me to make this pastoral visit to your country and to meet all of you. I wish to express cordial greetings also to those who have come from other African nations, particularly from the Republic of South Africa. It is fitting that the Church in Botswana should be represented here by members of the clergy, religious and laity. In communion with your bishop and with the Successor of Peter, you constitute a young and dynamic local Church. There is within your ranks a diversity of graces, ministries and works, but all these are brought into the unity of one body—the Body of Christ—by the power of the Holy Spirit. As the Second Vatican Council teaches us, "In the Church there is diversity of ministry but unity of mission" (*Apostolicam Actuositatem,* 2). All have a part to play in bringing Christ to the world.

In the reading we heard a few moments ago, Saint Paul speaks of his special calling as an apostle and his ministry as a preacher of the Gospel. He refers to his work as a "duty" and a "responsibility," for the sake of which he makes himself "all things to all men in order to save some at any cost" (cf. 1 Cor 9:16-23). And earlier in the same chapter he tells the Corinthians: "You are all my work in the Lord...you are the seal of my apostolate" (9:1-2).

342. It is within the context of the diversity of ministries in the Church, and of the special calling given to Saint Paul, that I wish to address my brothers and sisters who are priests or religious.

Dear friends, you are the spiritual heirs of Saint Paul and of all those missionaries who have given themselves without reserve in order to make Christ and his Church known and loved among the peoples of Africa. For the past *sixty years,* the Church in Botswana has been built up by the apostolic love and fervor of missionaries who have earned a warm and lasting remembrance in the hearts of the people of this country. These servants of the Gospel were men and women of faith whose lives confirm the tribute paid to religious in the Apostolic Exhortation *Evangelii Nuntiandi:* "By virtue of their religious consecration they are particularly free and willing to leave all things and go to the ends of the earth to preach the Gospel. They are always full of courage in their work, and their apostolate is often outstanding in its admirable resourcefulness and initiative. They are generous and are often to be found in the most remote mission stations where they may have to endure great dangers to health and even to life. Without doubt, the Church is *greatly indebted* to them" (n. 69).

The reality described by Pope Paul VI serves as a constant challenge to new generations of priests and religious who also wish to leave all things and follow in the footsteps of Christ. Inspired by the example of those who have gone before you, you too wish to *bear abundant fruit in the Church of today and the future.*

343. At this time, I would like to address a special word to *my brothers in the priesthood.* Like Saint Paul, you are servants of Christ and ministers of the Gospel. Through the sacrament of Holy Orders, you have been set apart to *act in his very person* and to *serve the priestly People of God.* In fulfilling this task, strive in a special way to help the *laity* of Botswana come to appreciate more deeply the importance of the *contribution they make* to the Church's mission. By living an active Christian life in the world, they bear witness to God's Kingdom and build up the Body of Christ. Particularly through the vitality of family life they make an invaluable contribution to the Church's mission.

344. The ordained priesthood and the priesthood of all the baptized *converge* in the *celebration of the Eu-*

charistic Sacrifice, which the Council describes as "the source and summit of all Christian life" (*Lumen Gentium,* 11). As I once wrote: "The priest fulfills his principal mission and is manifested in all his fullness when he celebrates the Eucharist, and this manifestation is more complete when he himself allows the depth of that mystery to become visible, so that it alone shines forth in people's hearts and minds, through his ministry" (*Dominicae Cenae,* Letter to Bishops for Holy Thursday 1980, February 24, 1980, n. 2). Dear brothers, may we always center our lives on this great mystery of faith which *reveals* to us the *true meaning* of our priestly vocation and is at the very heart of all our service to Christ and his Church.

345. I know that it is not always possible for you to celebrate the Eucharist with the faithful every Sunday. For that reason, dedicated extraordinary ministers of the Eucharist are available for communion services, and I wish to commend them for their generosity and faith. At the same time, it is important that *sound catechesis* be given concerning the extraordinary nature of these services in relation to the Mass, in order to ensure that the supreme value of the Eucharistic Sacrifice is not diminished.

Your task as brothers and collaborators with the bishop in shepherding the People of God also requires that you be "instructors in the faith" (*Presbyterorum Ordinis,* 6). In fulfilling this important responsibility, you necessarily rely on the generous collaboration of the many lay catechists in Botswana and you give them needed guidance and support. This is not meant to limit your own ministry of the Word but to make it more effective and fruitful. Together with the lay catechists, may you always experience the joy of bringing your people *to know and embrace the fullness of truth in Christ.*

The priest, my brothers, always has *an essential and personal role* in the ministry of "Word and sacrament." Many other demands are made on your time and energy, but it is especially in doing what is most essential to the priesthood that you find the *encouragement, strength and satisfaction* needed to persevere. May your daily prayer, too, bring joy to your ministry, so that the "peace of God which is so much greater than we can understand will guard your hearts and your thoughts, in Christ Jesus" (Phil 4:7).

346. I also wish to share some reflections with my *brothers and sisters in religious life.* Dear friends, while all the baptized share in the Church's mission, the Lord Jesus has called you to bear public witness to the Gospel in a way that sets you apart. Your religious consecration is a special source of spiritual vitality for the Church. It gives rise to a way of life that serves the People of God precisely by its fidelity to a particular charism and spiritual heritage. However, as I have said on other occasions, "even though the many different apostolic works that you perform are extremely important, nevertheless the *truly fundamental* work of the apostolate remains *always what* (and at the same time who) *you are* in the Church" (*Redemptionis Donum,* 15).

347. The Church depends on you to bear public witness to *the radical demands of the Gospel,* demands which are in danger of being obscured or ignored in today's world. That is why the religious habit is not without value in your apostolic service. Above all, the Church needs the joyful witness of your consecrated chastity, poverty and obedience. Your call entails a share in the *"folly of the cross,"* which will always remain a stumbling block to unbelievers, but in your own heart you know that the cross is truly the power and wisdom of God at work in those who believe (cf. 1 Cor 1:18 ff.). Thus, your love for the Crucified Lord is the basis of your vocation; your lives must be centered in him.

348. At the foot of the cross, beside the Mother of our Redeemer, you will also see the cost of *our reconciliation with God and with one another*. For, as Saint Paul says, those "that used to be so far apart from us have been

brought very close, *by the blood of Christ*" (Eph 2:13). Meditating on this great mystery, you will come to know more certainly that each of you and your whole communities must be *servants of this reconciliation in the world,* servants who can bring healing and peace to others because they have first of all experienced it themselves, especially through prayer and the sacrament of Penance.

349. By the *vow of chastity* you have become special *heralds of the resurrection of Christ and of the promise of eternal life.* You lift people's eyes beyond the demands of worldly affairs and the press of daily tasks, reminding them of the things that truly last. And yet, for the vow of chastity to be a compelling sign of the Kingdom to come, it must be inspired by a concrete *love for every one of God's children.* You are to "follow Christ by loving as he loved you, giving himself up in our place as a fragrant offering and a sacrifice to God" (Eph 5:2). By doing so you proclaim to the world that "God is love" (1 Jn 4:16), for his glory and for the salvation of all.

350. Your *vow of poverty* also proceeds from the love of God. With Saint Paul you can say: "For him I have accepted the loss of everything, ...if only I can have Christ and be given a place in him" (Phil 3:8-9). Detachment from material things enables you to be more *receptive* to the prompting of the Holy Spirit and more ready to receive his gifts. Through the practice of poverty, your lives stand as an *appeal for greater sharing* of the earth's resources, in a world in which relatively few people live in prosperity while many more struggle for the basic necessities of life.

The Second Vatican Council exhorts all religious to support the poor and to love them with the deep yearning of Christ. This theme was developed further by my predecessor Paul VI. For example, he said that the "cry of the poor" bars religious from whatever would be a compromise with any form of social injustice (cf. Apostolic Exhortation *Evangelica Testificatio,* June 29, 1971, 18). I know that this teaching strikes a responsive chord in your hearts, because you have witnessed *the plight of those who are subjected by law to discrimination.* And I gladly support you in your desire to be close to those who are unjustly deprived of their legitimate rights and lack decent living conditions. It is only fitting that, as followers of our crucified Savior, you would make great efforts to be in *solidarity with the poor and oppressed.*

351. And then, there is your *vow of obedience,* by which you have entrusted yourselves completely to God's designs in imitation of the Son of God who "humbled himself, even to accepting death, death on a cross" (Phil 2:8). You promised obedience to the Lord out of a firm conviction that God's plan for you is a plan of love. You were convinced that the best possible thing for you and for others is the faithful fulfillment of his will. In its concrete implementation this means the discernment of God's will within your religious community and *total* openness and *availability to the Holy Spirit* in the service of God's people. Through obedience you seek to lose your life in union with Christ and for the sake of the Gospel, precisely so that you may find your life through him (cf. Mt 16:25). A mature understanding of religious obedience prompts you to heed Christ's voice, even when it may seem that the path indicated is not the best for your own self-fulfillment or the use of your talents. But to those who love God, *all things work together unto good* (cf. Rom 8:28). Faith teaches us that "God's foolishness is wiser than human wisdom, and God's weakness is stronger than human strength" (1 Cor 1:25). (...)

The Holy Father here addressed the laity, then concluded as follows:

In your moments of discouragement and trial, never doubt that the Lord is near you. For he has called you by name. You are his. Trust in God to give you the grace you need to build up the Body of Christ through love and sacrifice.

May the grace and peace of our Risen Savior reign in your hearts.

25

TO PRIESTS, RELIGIOUS AND SEMINARIANS IN MASERU (LESOTHO)

September 15, 1988

352. "Ho rorisoe Jesu Kriste!"

Praised be Jesus Christ! It gives me great pleasure to greet you with that beautiful greeting which Blessed Joseph Gérard taught to his first converts and which has become an honored tradition among Catholic people of this country. Yes, praised be our Lord Jesus Christ! And praised be his Blessed Mother, especially today as we meet in this splendid church dedicated to her under the title of "Our Lady of Victories."

Dear brother priests, dear brothers and sisters in religious life and my dear seminarians: after having celebrated the Mass of Beatification this morning, I am very pleased to have this time, later in the same day, to be with you who are so dear to my heart. The *beatification of Father Joseph Gérard*, a priest and a religious, is truly a landmark in the history of Lesotho. It is *a sign of God's loving providence* at work in your midst. This is indeed a time to celebrate and give thanks to the Lord of history and the God of love who has called each of you by name and given you a share in his own divine life. And an important way of giving thanks to God is to recall the events of the past which have served as the channels of his blessings.

353. In the first place, we remember all the dedicated *missionary priests and religious of the past*—those men and women of strong faith and burning love who left behind their families and friends, their own cultures and homelands, to bring the Gospel of Christ to the beloved people of this land. Those pioneer missionaries traveled through the mountains of this beautiful kingdom, sowing the seed of the Christian faith and laying firm foundations for a strong and vibrant Church. The very memory of those

priests and religious calls to mind the words of the prophet Isaiah:

> *"How beautiful on the mountains are the feet of one who brings good news,* who heralds peace, brings happiness, *proclaims salvation"* (Is 52:7).

Indeed, "how beautiful the feet of one who *brings good news*"! And that is what priests and religious are called to do. We must be joyful heralds of the Good News of our Lord Jesus Christ. This is the rich heritage which is passed on to you today by the missionaries who have served in this land. Beginning with Father Joseph Gérard and his companions, the tradition of dedication to the preaching of God's Word and the work of total human development and liberation has been generously carried on by generations of priests and religious, most of them from foreign lands. To all those men and women of God we pay special tribute today. Through their labors, *the Church in Lesotho has experienced amazing growth,* in numbers and in works. The history of your country bears witness to the important contribution of priests and men and women religious, zealously working in many sectors of life, announcing Good News, heralding peace, bringing happiness, proclaiming salvation.

354. And now a new era is beginning in the life of the Church in Lesotho, *a new stage in the great task of evangelization.* It is a time marked by gratitude for the past and yet a readiness to face new challenges of the present and future, a time when the sons and daughters of Lesotho are now taking the place of many foreign missionaries, answering the call of Christ to carry on the Church's pastoral care in continuity with what has gone before. Like Saint Paul, *the missionaries "succeeded as an architect and laid the foundations,* on which someone else is doing the building" (1 Cor 3:10). The missionaries are still needed since they play an extremely important role, but it is right that ever greater responsibility should be

assumed by the native sons and daughters of this land. At the same time, I rejoice that the Church here is now sending missionaries, especially women religious, to other lands. This too proclaims the abundant fruitfulness of the love of Christ in your midst.

355. As the Second Vatican Council taught, "The work of planting the Church in a given community of people reaches *a kind of milestone* when the community of the faithful, already rooted in social life and considerably adapted to the local culture, enjoys a certain stability and firmness. This means that the community is now equipped with its own supply, insufficient though it be, of local priests, religious and laity..." (*Ad Gentes,* 19). The Church in Lesotho has reached this milestone with the help of God's grace and the efforts of many people. And the beatification of Father Joseph Gérard signals the attainment of a certain Christian maturity that proclaims the greatness of God's loving providence and the fruitfulness of divine grace at work in hearts that believe, a maturity that signals the local *growth in Christ.*

356. The Church in Lesotho, which has taken root so marvelously in this land, must now deepen the gift of faith and carry on the *unending task of evangelization,* particularly in those sectors which the Gospel has not yet reached. *The laity* must be helped to further the Kingdom of God in the ordinary events of daily existence. *The family* must be strengthened in unity and in its vital mission of life and love. *Society* must be uplifted and purified by the Gospel; social evils must be opposed and overcome, with justice and equality firmly established and secured by law. Then there are the special needs of *young people, the elderly, the sick and the disabled.* And the responsibility for this great enterprise falls, in a special way, upon your shoulders, my brothers and sisters in Christ, the priests and future priests, the men and women religious, whom God has called to serve him and his people in this land.

357. Remember the words of our Savior:

"You did not choose me,
no, *I chose you;*
and I commissioned you
to go out and to bear fruit,
fruit that will last" (Jn 15:16).

Christ has called you to be his "friends." Christ has sent you forth. Christ has entrusted to you the work of evangelization. Of course, every baptized person receives this charge and has a part to play. But in a particular way the Lord asks you, priests and religious, to *take the lead in proclaiming the Good News of salvation and in bearing public witness to the Gospel.* To you he says, as he said to the apostles: "Teach them to observe all the commands I gave you. And know that I am with you always; yes, to the end of time" (Mt 28:20).

358. Yes, *the Lord is with you always.* Never forget these reassuring words. May they be your consolation and your strength, your inspiration and your joy. The Lord is with you always, in whatever service you perform within the Church: in prayer, in the apostolate and in all your efforts on behalf of justice. Above all, the Lord is with you in the liturgical assembly. For this reason you must all be *men and women of the Eucharist.* For as the Church teaches: "The other sacraments, as well as every ministry of the Church and every work of the apostolate, are linked with the holy Eucharist and are directed towards it. For the most blessed Eucharist contains the Church's entire spiritual wealth, that is, Christ himself" (*Presbyterorum Ordinis,* 5).

359. In your communion with Christ you will find the strength to fulfill your mission in the Church. In Lesotho, as in any other country, this will mean an *evangelization of your culture,* that is, an evangelization of your customs and traditions, your Church's readiness for *a new era of* arts, your music, all those natural qualities and values that make up your society. All of these things

should be purified and enriched by the light and power of the Gospel.

360. But how does one evangelize a culture? How does one assist the work of the Holy Spirit in your midst? One begins by *evangelizing people,* for culture is produced by people and is shaped by the quality of the relationships that they have with one another and with God. And thus the *first step* is to evangelize as Jesus himself did, namely by *calling people to conversion.* Remember the first words of Jesus in his public ministry, as recorded in the Gospel according to Saint Mark: "The time has come," he said, "and the Kingdom of God is close at hand. Repent, and believe the Good News" (Mk 1:15).

361. The Christian life, in fact, entails constant conversion. A special help in doing this is the regular reception of the sacrament of Penance. Every aspect of our personal and social life must be *purified and inspired by the truth and love of Christ.* Only then can the laws and institutions of society be made to conform to the demands of justice and human dignity. It takes time to change attitudes and practices, but indeed they can be changed. With the help of God's grace and the power of Christ's death and resurrection, each of us can put on the mind and heart of our Lord and God.

362. Dear brothers and sisters in Christ: the mission you have received from God is indeed a vital one for the Church and for the world, a mission that will undoubtedly involve a share in the cross of Christ and at the same time a share in his risen life. As Saint Paul reminds us: *"It is all God's work.* It was God who *reconciled us to himself* through Christ and gave us the work of *handing on this reconciliation*" (2 Cor 5:18).

We must never forget this truth: "God reconciled us to himself." Our vocation began as God's work, God's gift of reconciliation and communion with himself. In grateful appreciation of this gift, make every effort to *preserve and deepen your union with God,* especially through daily prayer and a joyful imitation of Jesus in his chastity, poverty and obedience. This is the secret of a fruitful ministry in the Church; it is the path that Blessed Joseph Gérard followed in his long life of priestly service. Jesus himself has told us: "*Whoever remains in me, with me in him, bears fruit in plenty;* for cut off from me you can do nothing" (Jn 15:5).

363. Our communion with Christ will necessarily overflow in loving communion with one another. This is the commandment Jesus gave to his disciples: *"Love one another, as I have loved you"* (Jn 15:12). *Among priests,* there exists a special brotherhood rooted in their sacramental ordination. Thus it is only natural that they should love one another as brothers, support one another in the ministry of Word and sacrament, and make constant efforts to encourage one another through prayer, charity and mutual help.

364. Already in *the seminary* this spirit of priestly fraternity should have its beginning. Indeed, one of the purposes of priestly formation is to foster in each seminarian the human and spiritual qualities that will enable him to be an effective minister of reconciliation and a genuine brother in Christ to the other priests of his diocesan presbyterate.

365. Of course, *religious life* offers countless opportunities for growing in love not only of God but also of one another. Common prayer and a corporate apostolate are just two examples of ways that religious live a community life, rooted in mutual charity. Even more important for a deep spirit of brotherhood or sisterhood is the "oneness of mind and heart" that is fostered by their shared pursuit of holiness, their communal charism and their lifelong commitment to follow Christ in keeping with the Gospel and the Constitutions of their specific Institute.

366. As God's "chosen ones" and as servants of the Church, all of you, priests and seminarians, religious sisters and brothers, are called to *build up and strengthen the unity of all who believe in Christ.* Special efforts are at times needed to foster fruitful collaboration between the clergy and religious or between different religious Institutes. The laity must be accepted as true brothers and sisters in Christ, with a vital role in the mission of the Church and with a right to our friendship and encouragement. And no ministry in the Church can have lasting fruit if it is not carried out in faithful collaboration with the local bishop, in communion with the universal Church.

367. My brothers and sisters: I will close these remarks by making my own the exhortation of Saint Paul to Timothy: *"Fan into a flame the gift that God gave you....* God's gift was not a spirit of timidity, but the Spirit of power, and love, and self-control. So you are *never to be ashamed of witnessing to the Lord...* but with me, bear the hardships for the sake of the Good News, relying on the power of God" (2 Tim 1:6-8).

Never be ashamed of witnessing to the Lord!

Both in word and in deed, bear witness before the world to the Good News of our Lord Jesus Christ.

And may the Blessed Virgin Mary and Blessed Joseph Gérard help you by their prayers and heavenly protection.

God bless you all.

26

TO THE CLERGY, RELIGIOUS AND COMMITTED LAITY IN MAPUTO (MOZAMBIQUE)

September 18, 1988

368. It is a source of great joy for me to meet you whom the Lord "gazed at" with special delight. It was he who chose you and called you, so that, beginning with your *consecration in baptism,* you would renounce the world and, in a particular way, follow him more closely:

—some, *marked with the seal of the Holy Spirit,* to be consecrated for the divine worship, for the ministry of the Word and the service of the community: the priests;

—others, *to live exclusively for him,* "for the love of the Kingdom of heaven," in the freedom of those recognized as children of God, "lord" in relation to the world, and brother or sister to every other person, in dialogue and brotherly communion with them: the religious;

—and others, who exercise with special commitment the role which is theirs, the *mission of the entire Christian people,* in the Church and in the world: the laity.

To all of you I would like to propose the words of the apostle, which are a program in themselves: "freed from sin and having become slaves of God, your benefit is sanctification as you tend towards eternal life" (Rom 6:22), which testify to the fact that the world cannot be transfigured, nor offered to God without the spirit of the Beatitudes (cf. *Lumen Gentium,* 31).

369. I came to be with you to get to know you better and to show you that the *whole Church,* the Mystical Body of Christ, is *with you* and shares your problems and aspirations, your sufferings and hopes, *at a time* of profound transformation for this country. This brings with it *great changes*, not only external, but also with regard to the "soul" of the Mozambican people, whom we all love. To

them you want to announce the Gospel, so that they may, with the power of the Holy Spirit, purify themselves and affirm themselves fully, in their being and in their authentic values.

370. Your generosity and dedication have been guided by the pastors of the Church in this young nation, whose task it is to direct the whole ecclesial life in their own diocesan communities, discerning and harmonizing in a pastoral plan all the activities of those living a consecrated life (cf. *Mutuae Relationes,* 6) and, in turn, gathering the entire family of the flock and forming it, so that all may live and work in a communion of charity (cf. *Christus Dominus,* 16).

In greeting you, I would also like to greet your brothers and sisters scattered throughout Mozambique, expressing my esteem in Christ and wishing that all may continue "to listen to what the Lord God has to say: he *speaks of peace for his people* and for his faithful ones *and of hope* for those who turn to him in their hearts" (Ps 85 [84]:9).

371. I know that you are not discouraged by the many kinds of difficulties that you face: your small numbers, the dangers of war, the insecurity of your various situations, the scarcity of resources of all types. *Stronger* than all this is the love with which Christ loved you and the love of your response.

With you and for you I give praise and thanks to the God of all consolation and the Author of all good things, for the activity of your faith, for the efforts of your charity, and for the steadfastness of your hope, well founded in Jesus Christ (cf. 1 Thess 1:3). The witness that you give is, in fact, very consoling for me, in my concern for the whole Church.

372. Supported by the power of the Spirit, you want to be present to your brothers and sisters who suffer, *to be in solidarity with their suffering,* to share with them the

unfathomable riches of the love of God and to help them with the witness of "Christ in you, the hope of glory" (cf. Col 1:27). Neither do you hesitate to put yourselves on the *front lines of mission,* facing the greatest risks, including the risk to your very lives. We may well apply to you the words of *Evangelii Nuntiandi:* "In truth, the Church owes you a great deal" (n. 69).

In this sense, I cannot fail to *express my appreciation for the great work* you perform, that you realize here, in trying to incarnate the Church in the local culture, assuring essential services to the Christian communities, and giving them the structures necessary for their maintenance and development. Today, in an expression of ecclesial communion, this is realized through the presence and fraternal collaboration of distinguished missionaries from other nations; tomorrow, please God, with members of the local communities, fulfilling precisely what the Council desired in the solid implantation of the Church in a given human group (cf. *Ad Gentes,* 19).

373. Before addressing the various components of this select assembly, I would like to point out to everyone *two goals to have in view,* to animate and bring together all the efforts of pastoral charity and the apostolate:

—first, to be *heralds and artists of conversion,* in a broad sense: the change of mentalities serving values of a higher order, which are the common good and the full development of the whole person and of all people (cf. *Sollicitudo Rei Socialis,* 38); in this way you prepare the way for forgiveness and reconciliation;

—second, be witnesses and promoters of *reconciliation,* trying to *root out* of people's hearts all resentment and aversion. To accomplish this, pray "that all might come to know the truth and be saved" (cf. 1 Tim 2:4; 2 Pt 3:9); announce the *message of reconciliation* (2 Cor 5:19), preaching in season and out of season (2 Tim 4:2), in order to affirm "the unity of spirits, through the bond of peace" (Eph 4:3).

Only when these *two paths* have been traveled may we hope for the full realization of the promise of the psalm which we have just recited: "From the earth springs forth faithfulness, and justice looks down from heaven....Mercy and truth join hands and justice and peace embrace. The Lord will give his benefit and our land will yield its fruits" (Ps 85 [84]:11-13).

374. There is a fairly well-known formula born of the intuition of the People of God, which says: *the priest is an alter Christus.* It is not a metaphor; it is a marvelous and consoling reality, but one also indicative of tremendous responsibilities.

Direct collaborators in the episcopal ministry, by priestly *ordination* you entered into a kind of life that *distinguishes you in essence from the rest of the baptized;* by the "character" imprinted upon you, there was a transformation of the supernatural "organism" that enabled you to act "in persona Christi," to serve that love with which he surrounds the whole human family. It is a gift which, being *in you and not for you,* enriches you and calls you to grow in the consciousness and consistency of a real configuration to Christ, Priest and Good Shepherd.

375. "Established *on behalf of men,* in the things of God" (Heb 5:1), your ecclesial function is indispensable and well defined; it is neither a mere juridical appointment nor a delegation of the community. It is a life: *it is to live as if Christ were living in you,* and to reflect him constantly in your behavior, in your sacred ministry, in your service and in dealing with your brothers and sisters. All that you do should reveal your relationship to the Father in the Holy Spirit. The priest will never be able to be "another Christ" for people, if he is not first a "man of God" (cf. 1 Tim 6:11).

376. Here with you, I give thanks to the Most High for the sublime mission and ineffable confidence placed in you, for the benefit of the Church, of the Church in Mozambique, which, through the dedication of her priests, even amid tribulations, is always growing in numbers and

quality. Without ever becoming discouraged, put your trust in the living God, in *prayer* in all its forms, *centered in the Eucharist* and measured by the *Liturgy of the Hours,* always accompanied by authentic devotion to Our Lady, Queen of Apostles.

Your pastoral ministry, in communion with the bishop, demands the *perseverance, tact,* and *diligence* that are so well portrayed in the parables of the Kingdom (cf. Mt 13:1-51) and does not prevent your questioning yourselves, at times: "In the end, who am I?" The answer will be found in your faith and in your love of the Church: I am—as Mother Church teaches—called, consecrated, and sent out to be "another Christ," for all people, my brothers and sisters.

377. Due to well-known historical events, there is a *shortage of diocesan priests* in Mozambique. The vocations that reach ordination are very few. There are some signs of progress, thanks be to God! Without the hierarchical ministry, the laity, with all their goodwill, would not be able to carry out well their particular function. For this reason, we must hope and ask the Lord of the harvest for more and more Mozambican bishops and priests to assume responsibility and direct the destiny of the Church in this country.

It is more natural for you, my dear brothers, than for the dedicated missionaries, *"to have compassion on" the people of Mozambique,* to communicate and dialogue in their language, to understand their way of opening themselves up to God, and their customs. The impact of your witness and example will also be greater. May Jesus Christ—the perfect man, first fruit and ideal of the restored man, of the new man (cf. *Gaudium et Spes,* 22) in the divine and human dimensions of the mystery of Redemption—always be the model for your life and your work in the inculturation of the Gospel.

378. My dear brothers who are religious, a good part of whom are also priests—I would like to take some time to outline *your "profile"* as witnesses to the Beati-

tudes lived daily, as witnesses to the Absolute of God, to the invisible, and the life to come, to be lived in hope already, in the present; since that is not possible, I will simply apply to you the words of *Evangelii Nuntiandi:* "you are a privileged means of effective evangelization" (n. 69).

I cannot but emphasize the originality of your ecclesial state and its unquestionable value. Even when you dedicate yourselves directly to "pastoral" work, remain faithful to your place in the Church, which was defined well by the Second Vatican Council, and to the charisms which are proper to you. May all your activity, carried out with the diocesan clergy, be always, like the mission of the Son of God made man, a mission of love, peace, and redemption.

379. In you I see the glorious bands of religious who are so intimately connected with the history of the Church in this country; even today you make up the majority of the active clergy. To continue in your service, always producing more spiritual fruits for the sons and daughters of this land, I am sure that you will continue to develop peacefully, as you have so far, according to the spirit of the document *Mutuae Relationes,* the contacts, dialogues, and mutual understanding of your religious superiors with the bishops, who have been established by the Holy Spirit to govern the Church.

380. My dear women religious,

To you as well I want to express my esteem for the *gift* that you are *for the people of Mozambique,* who so greatly need the love of Mother Church, modeled as it is on the maternal affection of Mary, the Mother of Jesus. For some, "a great light has begun to shine"; others have not yet seen the "great light" of the "Prince of Peace" (cf. Is 9:1,6). This can happen through your witness of nuptial love for Christ, by which the *saving truth of the Gospel* becomes particularly visible among people; from it springs, as something proper to your vocation, that participation which you have in the apostolate of the Church, in her universal mission (cf. *Redemptionis Donum,* 15).

The witness of the total gift of yourselves to God, *to serve your brothers and sisters,* lived in chastity, poverty and obedience, makes of you a privileged expression of the Church herself to challenge society and the world. While remaining sensitive to the needs and sufferings of people, which are so clearly and movingly before your eyes, never forget: your *fundamental apostolate* remains *what you are in the Church,* according to the words of the apostle: "You have died, and your life is hidden with Christ in God" (Col 3:3).

381. The maturity and continuity of a particular Church also owes much to the consecrated life. In Mozambique, it is now a *time of great hope:* a consoling time that sees the flowering of women's vocations in the dioceses and the appearance of new Institutes also. These hopes will be confirmed if, in spite of immediate needs, there is a *profound and careful formation* of the new Mozambican religious within the *right framework:* a vision of faith, which nourishes generosity and perfection in charity, continued prayer-dialogue with God (cf. Jn 15:5), a deeply-rooted attachment to a particular Institute with its charism, and community life.

382. The *concrete model of life* that you offer, especially to young people, is in itself valuable—with your availability, detachment, competence and diligence—in working with communities, in teaching, caring for the sick, assisting the poor of all conditions, in promotion of women and of literacy. Always remember that, in all this, you must let the *gift of Redemption,* which is expressed in the evangelical counsels, *shine forth* as "living hosts, holy and pleasing to God" (cf. Rom 12:1): in a constant attitude of oblation. Be persevering in prayer, joyful in your dedication, and enthusiastic in your vocation!

383. I also wish to remember here those who live entirely consecrated to prayer, silence, and penance: the

religious of the contemplative life. They, too, are builders of the "city" of God, by what they are, being for people "signs" of redemptive love and enriching the pilgrim Church with a mysterious *apostolic fertility*.

I know that you, the *contemplatives*, are still very few in Mozambique. However, the Lord will provide. I am sure that initiatives will not be lacking, so as to second divine Providence and multiply your numbers.

384. To my dear *seminarians* and *aspirants to the consecrated life*, as well, I would like to extend a friendly greeting and a message: you have heard what I have just said to your elder brothers and sisters, those who have already tasted and seen how good the Lord is. You will not be surprised when the Church shows itself to be *attentive and even demanding* in regard to your formation and good preparation for the commitment that you wish to make conscientiously and generously. The Church is both a Mother and a Teacher and has a great deal of experience.

Learn to distinguish the voice of God and to deepen that most important "science," which is getting to know yourself and looking for *certainties* about that wonderful dream that you began early to dream: to give your life in total consecration to the Lord.

385. Like young Samuel (cf. 1 Sam 3:1-10), look for these certainties under the direction of your teachers. Establish an intimate dialogue, in prayer and meditation, with Christ, the "Good Teacher," (cf. Mt 19:16 ff.), who will enlighten you with the answer that you should give to God. Do not allow yourselves to be seduced by mere human interests. The consecrated person is not someone escaping from society, but rather someone who dedicates himself to society with even greater courage. The consecrated life, therefore, is an excellent way to serve your brothers and your country: *to serve* this dear *people of Mozambique*, who thirst for the truth and hunger for the "Bread of Life" (cf. Jn 6:48). (...)

27

TO MEN AND WOMEN RELIGIOUS AT MONT SAINTE ODILE, IN ALSACE

October 11, 1988

386. "Now we are all in the sight of God" (Acts 10:33).

It is with great joy that I meet you here on Mont Sainte-Odile, a place of special prayer and charity, a prestigious site in Alsace. Throughout the centuries it has seen the arrival of so many visitors and pilgrims, moved by the unique beauty of its glorious view, and interiorly regenerated by its truly spiritual atmosphere.

How can one help but experience a strong feeling of freedom, openness and growth before such an immense horizon? How can one not feel the call to find God in the silence of one's heart here where Odile, the great abbesses who succeeded her, and so many women religious have experienced his familiar presence? They wanted to present the truth and beauty of wisdom to as many people as possible, as is witnessed to in the famous work by Herrade of Landsberg, the *Hortus deliciarium*.

I give thanks to God that I could meet you here today, and I thank Providence for having led me in the footsteps of my distant predecessor, Leo IX, a native of this province, who consecrated this splendid mountain.

I greet you all most warmly. I greet you, nuns of the contemplative communities of Alsace, sisters engaged in teaching, in health care, in parishes and in missions. I greet you, priests, diocesan and religious. I greet you, lay adorers, who for almost three quarters of a century have taken turns night and day in uninterrupted prayer. I greet you, parishioners from neighboring parishes.

387. The Acts of the Apostles, from which the passage was just read to us, reports the beginning of the Church, with the freshness and dynamism which mark the birth of new works.

You also, sisters and brothers who belong to religious Institutes, have followed Christ with fervor and, after the example of the protagonists of the first evangelization of the world, you continue to keep your eyes fixed on the person of the *Risen Lord,* the way, the truth, and the life for all mankind. Like the apostles Peter and Paul, like the deacon Philip, you announce Jesus and proclaim that he is alive. You do it by the witness of your life of contemplative prayer, by your activities in the parish, by your devotion to the sick and the disabled, by your ministry as Christian teachers of youth in whom you inculcate a Christian vision of the world. Under your impulse, the adorers who pray day and night on this mountain also witness that Jesus is Lord and that to him alone belong praise and glory.

Following the apostle Peter, you say, in your own way, "what has happened throughout the land of Judea, beginning in Galilee with the baptism of John: Jesus of Nazareth has been consecrated by God with the Holy Spirit and filled with his power" (Acts 10:37-38).

388. I give thanks to God for the fruitfulness of the work of evangelization carried on by the sons and daughters of Alsace, which shines forth beyond the borders of the European continent and extends to numerous dioceses throughout the world. I encourage you to continue this proclamation of the Good News with the same quiet determination as that of the apostle Paul, of whom it is said in the last verse of Acts: "With full assurance and without any hindrance whatsoever, he preached the reign of God and taught about the Lord Jesus Christ" (Acts 28:31).

389. This full assurance is the gift that Christ gave to his Church on Easter Day, when showing himself to his disciples who were gathered together in the Upper Room, he declared: *"Peace be with you!"* As the Father sent me, so I send you" (Jn 20:21).

We have the mission of offering this peace of Christ

to a world that is in great need of it and that looks for it particularly from consecrated persons. In effect, you give the witness of a true personal life, which is the desire of every human being and which becomes more and more difficult in a mass society. You also give witness to a peaceful life, which attracts people who are searching for an existence that is ordered, unified, and stabilized by faith. People can find among you joy, self-giving, obedience, freedom, and the art of using well the things of this world. This makes your religious families so many little societies where the spirit of the Gospel reigns with the profound peace that comes from the practice of the Beatitudes.

390. This interior peace, a gift of the Risen Christ, is at the same time something you have won by walking the *demanding paths of chastity, poverty, and obedience.* What makes these ways of life "evangelical" is that you choose them precisely in order to follow Christ.

The choice that you have made of celibacy and perfect chastity is inseparable from faith in eternal life. In a world that finds it difficult to believe in the resurrection of the dead, you proclaim that the fullness of life is given to us beyond the passage of death and that this life is but a prelude to it. Did not Saint Augustine see in celibacy a sort of perpetual meditation on eternal life, since you already live it, but in a perishable body?

We can verify this: riches dull one's sensitivity to Christ's message. Did not Jesus proclaim that it is difficult for the rich to enter the Kingdom of heaven? By the simplicity of your way of life, which makes you practice a certain renunciation of temporal goods which fascinate our contemporaries, you remind them of the necessary detachment that all Christians must practice in order to invest fully in the Gospel values of love of God and neighbor.

Finally, at the cost of renouncing your own will, obedience develops in you a certain attitude of welcome that allows you to listen to those whom you go out to meet, and listen to those who come to you. Created in the image and likeness of God, a person should realize that doing God's will is not something frustrating, but rather, something that tends towards his or her development. In taking the path of the vows which leads to Easter peace, you are conscious of sharing in the cross of Christ, a way that surely leads to the resurrection.

391. You offer the Christian community examples of life that arouse its innermost support. Christians need the fidelity of your Institutes to be faithful themselves. They need your broad fraternity and ability to welcome in order to be fraternal and welcoming themselves. They need the example of your love, both within and outside your Institutes, to overcome the barriers of misunderstanding. They need your example of consecration to the values of the Kingdom of God in order to avoid the dangers of practical materialism. They need your vision of the Church's universality to remain open to the dimension of the world.

392. My dear brothers and sisters, you represent for the Church and for the world *great living forces.* You are witnesses of prayer. You announce the Gospel and you put people in contact with God through the sacraments. You support the ministry of the parish priest. You carry out the tasks of education, health care, and social services that correspond so well with the charity of the Church! You walk with the faithful in catechesis, in movements, and in missionary works. You do all this with great availability, and it is this fundamental disposition of openness to the love of God which makes you so useful. Helped by your vows, which deepen in you the capacity to welcome, you become more and more *capaces Dei*, which is the very vocation of the human person.

393. Finally, at the heart of your life, there is the *Eucharist,* adored day and night on this mountain. It is the Eucharist that nourishes your prayer and your action. You find there the strength of your consecrated life. You

recognize there the assurance of the truly transforming presence of the Risen Christ, who is with us until the end of the world....

28

TO THE GENERAL CHAPTER OF THE PASSIONISTS

October 14, 1988

394. I am happy to welcome and greet you all, Capitular Fathers of the Congregation of the Passion of Jesus Christ. In particular, I greet the Superior General, Father Paul Boyle, whom I thank for the words which he has just now addressed to me. You are assembled in Rome for the General Chapter; it is a particularly important time for the life of your Congregation. I accompany your work with my prayers, that the Lord may enlighten you and that you may respond to the problems and fundamental requirements regarding *the Institute's identity, as conceived by the Founder and repeatedly approved by the Church.* This is a task which you face in the light of the teaching of Vatican II, which in the decree *Perfectae Caritatis* offers to all an authoritative instrument for examination, comparison, correction and development. The "general principles" which it recalls for the "renewal of religious life" exclude *a priori* every possible equivocation inspired by a relativistic mentality, typical of the present culture, often agnostic and historicist. The Church conceives and encourages *progress only if it is geared towards a "constant return to the sources of the whole of the Christian life and to the primitive inspiration of the Institutes" (Perfectae Caritatis,* 2). The reason is obvious if one reflects that, for the Mystical Body, the most important measure of every human event is neither the "past" nor the "future" but the *present* of the eternal life of Christ, who emerges above all times as "the Alpha and the Omega, the First and the Last, the Beginning and the End" (Rev 22:13).

395. I know the seriousness with which, for centuries, you have guarded the patrimony of your Institute. The unqualified esteem of the faithful proves this; they have

always revered you for your austerity of life and the generosity of your missionary activity. Besides, clear confirmation is offered by the relatively high number of outstanding men who, faithful to the Founder's example, enjoy or are on the way to the honors of the altar. In this regard, I am happy to be able to add two Passionist Fathers, Berardo Maria di Gesù and Charles of Saint Andrew, to the list of the Blessed next Sunday.

396. Your Congregation is one of the Orders of mixed life, which, as the Council has indicated, "from their Rule or institution, unite the apostolic life with choral office and monastic observances" (*Perfectae Caritatis,* 9).

According to the charism of the sons of Saint Paul of the Cross, contemplation is fostered by solitude which is *also geographical;* this gives every house the character of a "retreat," and guarantees the religious a common life marked by specifically monastic observances, with silence and peace, conducive to "lofty abstraction from all creation," as your holy Founder expressed it.

397. However, there is more. That which distinguishes your spiritual life, the purpose of solitude, poverty, penance, is *that union with God, brought about by an intense participation in the expiatory and redemptive Passion of Christ.* This is so because it is in, and through the Savior's crucified humanity that, by achieving complete detachment from creatures, one can reach "the bosom of the Father," immersed in the mystery of his infinite love.

It is this life, "hidden with Christ in God" (Col 3:3), that distinguishes the contemplative profession of the Passionist, and, as it were, constitutes the *soul* of his activity in the Church, the inspiring motive of his dealings with the world. Here precisely is the *apostolic dimension* of his charism, *also characterized by the mystery of a Passion not only contemplated and lived, but also preached to the world as the "miracle of miracles of God's love"* (Saint Paul of the Cross).

398. On the occasion of your General Chapter, I wish to recall these typical aspects of Passionist spirituality, because they are indispensable premises for any reflection on the past and for every possible proposal for the Congregation's future renewal.

You are all aware how your "identity as contemplatives and apostles of Christ Crucified" is exposed today to currents which are destructive of thoughts and customs. It is a question of forces which can disorientate even the most watchful, because they appear to be justified by the very elements which are essential to the nature of the Institute, interpreted *in a reductive sense,* and very often *out of the context* which forms the synthesis of the *way of thinking and acting peculiar* to the Founder and the many saints who have graced your Congregation.

399. Therefore, I exhort you not to yield to the "temptations" of our time.

I refer in particular to the difficult synthesis of the two elements, the *contemplative* and *active,* since Paul of the Cross founded an Institute of *contemplative apostles* who from the very richness of a greater concentration on God drew the power to spread throughout the world.

The mystery of the Passion gives you a name and, like your distinctive religious habit, sets you apart from all the other Orders. Consequently, none of you can take up secular professions or start his own movements of spirituality or become promoters of experiences inconsistent with the specific nature of the vocation professed by your Institute; this would be a betrayal of the Founder's original charism.

400. *Solitude, poverty,* and *penance*—aimed at union with Christ in God, and forming you into the contemplative solicitous for his personal sanctification—must enkindle in you the zeal which breaks forth in missionary activity. This missionary activity is *not generic* but *specific,* because it is limited to the *ministry of the Word* and proclaims a "wisdom of the Cross" assimilated in the silence of the retreat, in the austerity of the common life, in the

deliberate rejection of every profane distraction.

This throws light on the sound tradition of alternating periods of recollection and rest "at the feet of Christ Crucified" with periods of apostolic work carried out *according to very definite forms* of special preaching which owe their irresistible impact to the contemplative reserves accumulated in the quiet of the monastic life.

Certainly, you cannot remain insensitive to the many needs of the Church and to the diversified demands of new social categories. However, that requires merely adaptation, not the *suppression* of the traditional *ministry of the Word,* replacing it by forms of activity which would force you to sacrifice the contemplative dimension of your vocation, the only real secret of all missionary work.

To you, perhaps more than to any other category of religious, the Council repeats that "even the best-contrived adaptations to the needs of our time will be of no avail unless they are animated by a spiritual renewal, *which must always be assigned primary importance even in the active ministry"* (*Perfectae Caritatis,* 2e).

I hope that these reflections will encourage you to a process of renewal capable of revealing the perennial vitality of the Institute to a world awaiting intrepid men to proclaim the "wisdom of the Cross" through the witness of their life and word.

With these heartfelt wishes, I impart my blessing to you and extend it to all the members of your Congregation.

29

TO THE GENERAL CHAPTER OF THE HOSPITALLER ORDER OF SAINT JOHN OF GOD

November 25, 1988

402. I welcome you most cordially, representatives of the Hospitaller Order of Saint John of God, during this brief pause in the work of your General Chapter, which is being held at an important time in the history of health in the world in which we live. (...)

I hope that you may draw abundant spiritual fruits from your meetings for the good of your entire Order, founded to give glory to God through serving the sick. We know that every General Chapter is always an event of great importance, because it not only allows one to take a look at the overall progress of the religious life according to the particular founding charism, but also serves to arouse new spiritual fervor and a more generous dedication to one's ideal. For you, members of the worthy Order popularly and significantly known as *Fatebenefratelli,*[1] it is mostly a question of interiorizing the sense of *Christian hospitality* which you all profess with a special vow in the Church. Your Constitutions prescribe a specific commitment "to defend and watch over a person's right to be born, to live decently, to be assisted in infirmity and to die with dignity," so that "it is always clear that the center of interest is the needy or sick person" (n. 23).

403. Great tasks await you, dear brothers, and the Church asks you to perform them in the spirit of the Lord's words: "As you did it to one of the least of these my brethren, you did it to me" (Mt 25:40). It is in these words that you must find the basis of your concept of "service."

The Council, particularly in the first part of *Gaudium et Spes,* has fully emphasized the importance and dignity of serving the sick. A theology of service can be proposed insofar as the Church shows herself as a society of Christ's disciples who are qualified and distinguished by their mutual help and love.

In today's complex society you must distance yourselves, if necessary, from old practices, and search for a model of a "theology of service" as a courageous step leading you to invent something new. In a way more and more in keeping with the times, you are called to rethink the fundamental relation between the Christian faith and the forms of charitable service.

404. Your way of witnessing to the faith will be all the more effective to the extent that it is founded on the capacity to go out from self in order to be open to the suffering, poverty, and needs of others.

Solely in this openness does your service have reason to exist, aiming at practical aid to others rather than a formal project of assistance. I think that theological reflection can no longer be separated from practical organization of service.

Thus the sick, the suffering and the needy—who at times are an inconvenience, almost a hindrance, to some people—become the persons most cherished by the one who has faith, because they are living signs of God's presence. To make room for another, to exercise the charism of hospitality, in a certain sense means to make room for Christ and make him live with you and in you.

405. Your community of brothers at the service of the sick is fully realized in the evangelic *diakonia* which must always animate your work. On this also you must base your witness before your lay colleagues, who from a merely professional involvement in health care can arrive at a service conceived as an expression of love and Christian solidarity.

Your communities can and should aim at building that "social space" needed by the new sick, whom advanced technology can no longer help and for whom the large institutions are useless. I am thinking, for example, of AIDS victims, cancer patients, or of psychiatric patients.

Your communities must become the reference point in safeguarding the rights of the human person and respect for individual freedoms. May your activity in the service of the needy inspire you, above all, to a practical faith which is essential and turned toward the one thing necessary: the Kingdom of God of which Jesus speaks, in the hope that the rest will also be given to you (cf. Mk 6:33).

406. Those who suffer and towards whom you exercise your compassion have much to teach you for the transformation of your existence as religious; let the sick person be your university!

You will effectively witness to your identity as Hospitaller Brothers of Saint John of God if you base every program on real, existing needs; if you give preference to the person who is suffering; if you do not rely solely on individual opinions not in perfect harmony with the original charism which has produced noble examples of true *servants* of the sick, and whose names are held in honor.

407. I cannot forget that in this ideal of service, imitating the generosity of your Founder, you are seeking to bring your model of Christian hospitality to developing countries also. Do not neglect their cultures, listen to their real needs, bring to all, beyond ethnic differences, the same witness to Christ, dead and risen. Thus the Church can begin, grow and coexist also where there are other religions and other lifestyles.

With this commission to love and be in solidarity with our weakest brothers, I express my best wishes for a fruitful continuation of the work of your General Chapter, so that the whole Order will acquire the impulse necessary to continue in its way which is so inspiring and meritorious.

I cordially bless you and your entire religious family.

---

[1] Name given in Italy to the Hospitaller Brother of Saint John of God, literally, "You do good, brothers."

30

TO THE PLENARY ASSEMBLY OF THE CONGREGATION FOR RELIGIOUS AND FOR SECULAR INSTITUTES

December 1, 1988

408. A cordial greeting to all of you. I thank you for your visit on the occasion of your plenary assembly, which has "formation in religious Institutes" as its theme.

I thank Cardinal Jerome Hamer for his introduction to this meeting. I am pleased with the choice of subject, which is most important. Indeed, it is necessary to emphasize that formation of religious must aim especially at *wisdom of the heart,* that gift of the Spirit which makes one truly intimate with the Lord and enlightened to know his will. This wisdom contributes much more to the salvation of the world than a multiplicity of external activities not animated by the supernatural spirit.

409. The eyes of many of our contemporaries are justly turned towards the sad living conditions of so many human beings who lack the minimum necessities of life, and therefore towards the urgent and necessary demands of human justice and dignity. Now, without denying the timeliness and necessity of the commitment of religious in this vast area of human solidarity, in particularly serious situations, it is necessary to bear in mind that the characteristic proper to the mission of the consecrated person is, as the Council says, to show "more clearly to all believers the heavenly goods which are already present in this age, witnessing to the new and eternal life which we have acquired through the redemptive work of Christ and foretelling our future resurrection and the glory of the heavenly kingdom" (*Lumen Gentium,* 44).

410. Everyone knows that the *role of religious superiors,* especially major superiors, in the formation of the

members of their Institutes *is important and indispensable.* It is they who admit the candidates and choose qualified directors of formation. Also, they are bound to see to the drawing up of a formation program (*ratio institutionis*) and a plan of studies (*ratio studiorum*) in accordance with the law. They receive the religious profession of novices and professed; they obtain for those finally professed the "assistance and the time" (can. 661) to be "diligent in continuing their spiritual, doctrinal and practical formation" (*ibid.*).

I think that the list of these duties is in itself sufficiently eloquent to dispense me from insisting further on these important aspects.

411. It is obvious from this that the duty of the formation director—and of the superior, in the first place—requires an *adequate preparation.* Over and above technical or professional qualifications it is necessary to pay attention to spiritual qualities; you know this. Indeed, only those who are themselves enlightened and wise can form the wise. Besides, the task of formation director presupposes outstanding human qualities and a combination of spiritual gifts which makes it possible "to build in Christ a fraternal community, in which God is sought and loved above all" (can. 619).

412. It is also important to *choose and prepare formation directors* with great care. The mission which they must carry out is indeed particularly delicate. It requires respect for persons, attention, firmness, and enlightened understanding.

Your Congregation has already offered guidelines on this matter in the document on the contemplative dimension of religious life. I hope that they will be the object of reflection by the superiors of Institutes, so that they can draw benefit from them for their task.

413. In the formation cycle in religious life, *the beginning* merits special attention; first of all, so that only

those candidates are admitted who possess the qualities necessary to profit fully from it. In view of the situation of young people today, and the deficiencies frequently found in family and scholastic life, it is not always easy to find all the required qualities combined. However, one can accept into the novitiate those young people who have given proof of a certain maturity from the standpoint of religious knowledge, sacramental practice and ethical behavior.

414. The superiors of Institutes should not neglect to provide also a well-organized *ongoing formation.* Therefore I wish to repeat here what I have already said to the religious of Brazil: "All religious Institutes have the duty to prepare and carry out an adequate plan of permanent formation for all their members. This program must aim not merely at intellectual formation, but at that of the whole person, particularly *in the spiritual dimension;* in order that every religious can live fully his particular consecration, in the specific mission entrusted to them" (*Insegnamenti di Giovanni Paolo II,* IX, 2, 1986, p. 251).[1]

415. However, I do not want to forget the formation of *contemplative* religious. Their spiritual and apostolic fruitfulness within the Church is great, in proportion to their total self-giving to the Lord. However, in order that their fruitfulness can be realized and lived by each of them, it is necessary to have an appropriate formation which is at the same time doctrinal, liturgical and ascetical, not to speak of the human balance—especially psychological—demanded by the routine of their lives, their permanent separation from the outside world, and the prolonged periods which they must devote to prayer and study.

416. Finally, I mention the *foundation of new Institutes* and the formation given to their candidates. Your Congregation, in collaboration with the Congregation for Bishops, has published an important docu-

ment which has already borne much fruit and is destined to have a lasting influence on the mutual relations between bishops and religious, in a Church considered as an "organic communion" (*Mutuae Relationes,* 5).

This document provides sure criteria and useful directives for the foundation of new Institutes, in a certain way recalling the prescription of *Perfectae Caritatis,* (n. 19) and *Ad Gentes* (n. 18), which ensure the solid base of an authentic and specific charism for every foundation.

Therefore I insistently remind the founders and responsible bishops of "the duty of caring for religious charisms; all the more so because the very indivisibility of the pastoral ministry makes them responsible for the perfection of the entire flock" (*Mutuae Relationes*, 9), having recourse to these criteria and directives. The mission of religious life in the Church depends very much on this.

417. I entrust these thoughts and wishes to the Blessed Virgin Mary, "the first among all persons consecrated to God" (cf. *Redemptionis Donum,* 17). At the same time, I invite religious to renew the grace of their "religious consecration according to the model of the consecration of the Mother of God herself" (*ibid.*).

I willingly impart my special blessing to all.

---

[1] Cf. Book IV, n. 362.